MW01700622

The Wealthy Home Seller

What will you do with the money you save?

Dale Betts

GlenMargaret
PUBLISHING

1st printing December 2006

editing by Bronwen Hook
text layout by Richard Rogers
cover layout and design by Hudson Studio

All characters in this book are fictitious. Any resemblence to actual persons, living or dead, is purely coincidental.

Printed in Canada

Library and Archives Canada Cataloguing in Publication

Betts, Dale, 1971-
The wealthy home seller / Dale Betts.

Includes index.
ISBN 0-920427-78-2

1. House selling—Canada. 2. Real estate business—Canada.
I. Title.

HD1379.B48 2006 643'.120971 C2006-906174-2

This book is dedicated to all home sellers who want to retain the equity they worked so hard to build.

Acknowledgements

This finished product acknowledges the tireless contributions of those who have done so much to make the success of this project and PropertyGuys.com possible. Without Dale Betts grinding away like the steady defensive defenceman he is, the manuscript may never have been completed and could have just lay around gathering dust, buried by the many other pressing issues of the day. Dale's attention to detail and his ability to take a project all the way through to completion are his greatest strengths and we are thankful that he brought those skills to the table in Bobby Orr style.

But a team is not made of one man. There are always others making passes, taking hits, and setting up the big plays. And this effort was no different. Ken LeBlanc, Walter Melanson and Jeremy Demont worked side-by-side with Dale as each of the chapters was laid out to tell the story of how selling a home is changing; how today's home seller can keep the hard-earned equity they have built up in their home. Let's not forget the efforts of our road warrior Matt Eldridge who has spent countless hours of adding key franchise owners across the country to our team.

This book represents the collective thoughts, ideas and real life experiences of these five champions of the real estate revolution.

Finally, it would be remiss not to mention the hard

work and dedication of the entire PropertyGuys.com franchise group; a group that is dedicated to educating home sellers on the benefits of selling privately.

What will you do with the money you save?

Foreword

It started with 98 dollars and an idea they couldn't shake....

In 1998, during the fall semester at university, two undergraduate students sat in the library, surrounded by testaments to the success of others, tackling an assignment, unaware of the rumbling implications for their own destiny. Books lay open, binders piled on the table; one of them tugged at a lock of hair while the other tapped a notebook with a pen. One would speak, both would lean forward in excitement, then the flaw in the idea was discovered, and they relaxed their posture again. Over and over they came back to the question assigned by their business professor: "*What need could you address with a new business, and how would you structure it in line with management principles?*"

Across the lawns outside the library, trees painted shadow self-portraits with absurdly long trunks as the sun dipped towards the horizon. Students walked, laughed, played, thought, and romanced in the cool fall air. Still in the library, the pen tapped, the lock of hair slipped between nimble fingers. One of them started speaking; again the alert posture but, this time, no relaxation followed.

"What if we started a business that helped people sell their houses without a real estate broker?"

Quonk! The pen is still, and the hair forgotten. They

quickly checked the idea for flaws, found none, and felt new excitement drive exhaustion from their minds. A business that helped people sell their homes without a broker – that's new! And a viable concept! That day in the library, the two students found the topic for their life's calling. PropertyGuys.com was born that day, a new idea conceived in an atmosphere rich with the legacy of past great thinkers.

Business 101 was their introduction to Reality 101, forging a link between idea and implementation.

"What if we knocked on the doors of people, found those who want to sell their home privately, and took pictures with our 35 mm to load on a web site? How would that help, and what more could we do?"

Coupled to the concept of do-it-yourself home sales, ideas came one after another, until the two students had an entire train of action. Sure, there were spaces to be filled, such as where to get signs, and just how much information a home owner needed to make the sale. Yet the train was ready to leave and, with just $98, Ken Leblanc and Jeremy Demont left the station, laying the tracks for Canada's largest private home sale network.

Right from the beginning, PropertyGuys.com dared to play the role of both revolutionary and pioneer in terms of turning the traditional real estate industry upside down by asking one simple question: *"How can we make the entire real estate transaction focused more on the customer, allowing them to protect their equity rather than lining the pockets of a middleman?"*

PropertyGuys.com has never stopped asking this type of question. The kind of question that is totally focused on their very reason for being; their customers. Homeowners who want to sell privately.

And they are doing it once again with the release of this, their first book. *"The Wealthy Home Seller"* represents another step in what has been referred to as "the real estate revolution", as PropertyGuys.com aims to radically change an industry establishment that blocks many homeowners from realizing the power they have to sell without a real estate broker. All these homeowners really need is, to quote the Beatles, "a little help from their friends": support by professional marketing materials, and the massive power of the internet. Once these tools were provided, it was only a matter of time before a common sense revolution took place within the real estate sector as thousands upon thousands of home sellers found out for themselves just how easy it can be to put a few more thousand dollars back into their pocket.

The key to this sweeping change in the marketing of real estate is the internet. Similarly, the internet has allowed companies like Expedia and eBay to transform travel and the auctioning of second-hand items. This new technology has created unlimited possibilities for consumers who want to do things for themselves whether it's booking a flight or a hotel room, or buying concert tickets, stocks and bonds.

By reading *The Wealthy Home Seller,* anyone thinking of selling a home privately will learn just how easy and profitable it can be. The story is a fictional account of a private sale transaction and how neighbours chatting in their backyard come to realize the many advantages of doing it on their own.

The title of the book and the story it tells is also a way of paying homage to one of Canada's most recognized authors and speakers, David Chilton. Just as Chilton's *"The Wealthy Barber"* demystified financial planning for those who don't consider themselves experts, this story takes us on a similar journey with characters you will quickly recognize.

Enjoy the story; but more than that allow yourself the opportunity to benefit from the wisdom that is revealed in these pages. *The Wealthy Home Seller* story is played out in thousands of communities just like yours.

Who knows? This might become your story one day.

Gair Maxwell,
Fundy Business Institute, October 2006

Contents

1
The Conversation

It's a beautiful fall afternoon as Tom Allen steps out his back door, onto his deck and down the steps to his yard to begin raking the leaves that he's let accumulate for over a week. He has pulled himself away from the college football game on television to take care of a chore that has been on his list for a couple days. Tom enjoys the outdoors and likes puttering around the yard once he finally gets out there. The first step is always the most difficult, but once he gets going, he can't be stopped.

Tom likes to think of himself as handy, but often doesn't know where to start. Like many, he is much handier when he has people around him that actually know what they're doing. This year, Tom's big project was his back deck. He took on the once-believed overwhelming task of building onto his existing deck to make it considerably larger. Tom loves to barbeque in the summer, but his once small, cramped, little deck didn't offer nearly enough room for his friends and family to sit out and enjoy their food under the warmth of the summer sun. The new addition to the deck worked out perfectly for the end of summer get-together he hosts each year.

Speaking of family, Tom and his wife Julie are expecting their second child. Their first child, Billy, is almost 3 years old. He was just a newborn when Tom and Julie first moved into the house. While the smaller sized split entry offers plenty of room for the three of them, the house will feel a little smaller once the fourth member of the family arrives.

As Tom walks down the stairs, off the deck, toward the unkept lawn that he was about to make right, he pauses for a moment to reflect on his handy work. As he grabs the rake that he left leaning on the side of the house a couple weeks earlier, he hears his neighbour, Walter, call out, "Great looking deck, Tom". And Walter would know.

Walter Williams is the neighbour everyone wishes they had: a wizard when it comes to home improvement. There doesn't seem to be a household job that Walter doesn't know how to tackle. Need a wall knocked down, a sink pipe changed, some electrical work done? Walter's the guy. He can also build just about anything.

Truth be known, Walter's support was what gave Tom the courage to actually tackle building his own deck. Early in the spring, once the weather was beginning to warm up, Tom mentioned to Walter that he'd love to expand his deck, but didn't think the cost of getting someone in to do the job was in the budget. He wished it was, but he didn't think he could quite swing it.

Over the next few weeks, Tom seemed to mention this new deck every time he and Walter crossed paths. Since Walter knew the cost of the wood was probably affordable, Walter finally said to him, "You keep talking about this deck. Let's go get the wood and do it ourselves."

Tom liked this idea. By working on the deck with Walter, he was able to cut out the cost of the carpenters and make the project financially possible. With no labour costs other than a few cold drinks for Walter when he was over, this cut the entire cost of the deck in half; a considerable savings for Tom.

Tom and Julie are fairly cost conscious when it comes to their finances. While they don't seem to ever go without anything, or at least very rarely, like many people these days, they don't have a lot of extra money sitting around either. They are always looking for ways to stretch their annual income. Tom, especially, gets very curious when he learns of new ways to save money.

Tom and Walter have grown fairly close over the years they have been neighbours. Interestingly enough, their relationship began when Tom dropped by soon after they had moved in to borrow Walter's circular saw after the blade on his had broken. Tom was building some wood shelves for storage space in his baby barn. Walter offered to help him, and that's where Tom learned just how talented Walter is. Since that time, Walter has served as a mentor to Tom with respect to do-it-yourself projects.

Walter has this uncanny ability to take on just about any project, boil it down to its bare essentials and make it simple. Tom has grown to enjoy the time he spends with Walter, and over the years some of Walter's skills have rubbed off on his neighbour; although Tom still likes the comfort of having Walter helping him with some of the more challenging tasks.

"Sure love the job we did on this deck, Walter. I can't thank you enough for all your help," Tom calls back as he heads toward Walter's yard with the intent of striking up a quick conversation and delaying his yard work for just a little while longer.

The short walk over would be eye-opening. As he reaches his neighbour's yard, Tom catches a glimpse of a "For Sale" sign out of the corner of his eye. Tom gives a double take to make sure his peripheral vision wasn't playing tricks on him. Sure enough, it wasn't.

"Walter, what is that on your front yard?" Tom asks, surprised.

Walter and his wife Carole are entering their empty-nest years. Their last child has just started his second year of university, while another one is in their final year. Both of them attend school out of town and have been finding summer jobs near their schools during the summer. The other two children have graduated and are out on their own. His oldest daughter and her family live in town; Walter still likes seeing them regularly. But the house has just got too big for him and Carole. They will be looking for something a little cozier now that it's just the two of them.

Before Walter can even answer, Tom follows up: "Are you really selling your house?"

"I'm glad you came over Tom," Walter said in a comforting tone. "We wanted to let you and Julie know that we were putting our house on the market. We just put the sign up this morning and knew that the two of you might find it a bit of a surprise. We were going to call you later today."

Not only have Tom and Walter grown close since they've been neighbours, but their families have as well. Two winters ago, the two couples headed south for a week-long vacation. Tom and Julie were able to leave their one year old Billy at Tom's parents place across town. The Williams' youngest son, while still in high school, living at home at the time, enjoyed the freedom of being home by himself, although Carole's father dropped in once in awhile to make sure it wasn't a week long dorm party.

Come to think of it, it was just prior to this trip that Tom realized just how big of a "do-it-yourself" kind of guy Walter really was. Tom knew he was adept at tackling home and yard projects, but this vacation planning session would open Tom's eyes to how technology could also help and empower the "do-it-yourselfer".

As the two couples were discussing the trip and how they would book the flights, accommodations and rental cars, Walter volunteered to take care of it. He said that they could each save a few hundred dollars if he went and booked all these necessities over the internet. Online travel companies allowed vacationers to find their own hotels, car rentals and attractions at a more favorable price. Instead of monies being paid to travel agents, the savings were passed along to the vacationer.

At the time, this was a revelation to the Allens. Although they were not ones to take many vacations, the couple of times they did get away, they had always used a travel agent to line up their plans. This was a new approach for them. Walter presented the group with a number of different possible itineraries, all at a reasonable price. Tom couldn't believe the price of the packages Walter put together. The savings were impressive.

Tom and Walter carry on their conversation as they walk toward the front of the house where the 'For Sale' sign is firmly planted. Walter continues: "We've been talking about selling for the last year or so. We think it is time to downsize a bit. It just doesn't make economic sense to be in a house this big when it's just the two of us here most of the time."

When they reach the front of the house, Tom notices something peculiar about the sign. It's not a traditional real estate company sign; there is no real estate agent's picture or name on it. It's a professional looking sign, but it has PropertyGuys.com on it, and the prominent words "Private Sale". The sign has Walter's phone number on it. This strikes Tom as odd.

"Walter, I've never heard of PropertyGuys.com. Are they a new real estate company in town? And why is your phone number on the sign?" Tom asks curiously.

"Well, PropertyGuys.com is not your traditional real estate company; they're actually a national real estate marketing company that helps people sell their own homes," Walter explains, "When I did a little research, they were by far the best private sale company I came across. They do all the marketing to get my home in front of potential buyers, and I get to stay in control of the rest.

"And while they are a national company, they have local people that helped set me up and are available to answer any questions I might have. It's great, because they can guide me through all the steps of selling my house.

"See, Carole and I have decided to sell our home privately this time. No agents. My phone number is on the sign because as a private seller, I want people interested in my home to contact me to discuss the sale," Walter states confidently. "We are going to market and sell our home on our own, with the help of PropertyGuys.com."

"Can you really do that?" Tom asks inquisitively. "Don't you need a real estate agent to sell a house? I always thought people only sold on their own when agents wouldn't accept their listing; when there was something wrong with the house. Is there something wrong with your house?"

Walter chuckles. "No, no, no, there is nothing wrong with our house," he replies still grinning. "In fact, I can almost guarantee that the first three or four people to call the number on the sign will be real estate agents wanting to list it.

"Listings are extremely valuable to real estate agents because as the selling agent, once they list a house, they get at least a split of the commission whether or not they actually find the buyer.

"And some agents will try almost anything to get your listing. A lot of agents will tell you that they have buyers already lined up for your house even before it's listed. Or they'll tell you that if your house doesn't sell in so many days, that they'll buy it from you. You should read the fine print on that contract!

"I had one agent call me up the last time I sold my home on my own and asked me if I would list my house with him. When I said no, he told me that I must not be really interested in selling my home.

"With the average commission between 5-6% of the selling price, each listing is worth thousands of dollars to them. We want to keep those dollars in our pockets. We have sold privately before, and are quite comfortable doing it. There are a lot of people that don't realize that selling a home is not all that difficult and that it can be done without an agent."

Tom is one of them. He hadn't realized that selling a home privately was an option; or that Walter had done it before. Recognizing that his family is growing and he may be faced with selling his own home in the next few years, Walter's choice of selling privately piques Tom's curiosity.

"Why would you want to sell your own home when there are real estate agents that will do it for you? Isn't it difficult to sell your own home?" Tom inquires.

And there it is. The two most frequently asked questions when it comes to selling a home privately. But Walter knows the answers; he's lived the answers. "You know what Tom, those are good questions. Let me tell you about what happened the last time we sold a home. I think you might find this interesting."

"Before we moved into this house, Carole and I lived across town by the lake. We wanted to move to this side of town to be closer to work, so we put our house on the market with an experienced real estate agent. As part of the deal, we were going to use the same agent to buy our next house also. He would act as our selling agent for our existing home and our buying agent for our new home. We were excited at the prospects of selling our home and moving across town. This agent had been in the business for over a decade and had a good number of listings all over town.

"It wasn't too far along in the process that we began to see some oddities in the agent system. Over the first few weeks that we had our house listed, our agent held an open house on the weekends and there were a reasonable number of people through our house. After the first two or three weeks though, this activity died down quite a bit. Our agent no longer seemed as excited about our listing. Carole even pointed out that he wouldn't always highlight the key selling features of the house when he would bring people through. We were surprised by this.

"Even more interesting was what would happen when prospective buyers working with other agents wanted to see the house. The buying agent would sometimes call wanting to see the house immediately because they happened to be driving around the neighbourhood. The buying agent would contact our selling agent who would then contact us to see if we could leave for a bit; it felt like we lost control of our schedule. Of course we couldn't just refuse potential buyers.

"To make matters worse, when this buying agent brought his clients into our home, he wouldn't be familiar with our house. There were two or three occasions when we saw different agents we had never seen before pull up to the house as we were leaving to allow them to show it. Since it was the first time the agent had been through our house, we're still not sure what was said to those prospects.

"After having been listed for a few months with little activity towards the end, the agent approached us and suggested we should lower the price of our house if we wanted it to sell. Well, Carole and I knew we needed to get a certain amount of money for our house to make the move financially smart, but with the lower price our agent was suggesting, we would be under that targeted amount once the commission was paid from that total; we just couldn't do it.

"At the same time, I had been noticing private sale signs and 'For Sale by Owner' signs around; so I looked into them a little further. While I didn't have any formal training in real estate, I knew selling privately was something I could do. I approached the agent and told him that we couldn't lower our price to the level that he would have liked, and I suggested that we terminate the contract so he wouldn't have to worry about my listing, and I wouldn't have to drop my price. We both agreed.

"I wasted no time switching the real estate agent's sign to a 'For Sale by Owner' sign and with the first phone call I received from an interested buyer, I quickly recognized the first advantage of selling a home privately; control. I dealt directly with the person interested in my house. I could set the day and time of the appointment. And when they arrived, I could highlight the features of the home I knew to be important. Nobody knew the house better then Carole or me.

"Once we closed the sale of our home, we recognized the second major advantage to selling a home privately; savings – real dollar savings. With real estate agents charging anywhere from 5% commission and up, the realties of writing a commission check become scary. Add tax to the commission and the amount is even greater.

"Eliminating commissions from the sale of a home can save a home seller thousands of dollars, even ten's of thousands of dollars depending on the selling price. When you consider the 5% as a percentage of total equity in a home, it's easy to see why private sale home sellers could be called 'wealthy home sellers'; because they are protecting their wealth by protecting their equity. Think of all the things you could do with that kind of money.

"We saved well over fourteen thousand dollars on the sale of that house," Walter continued, with excitement in his voice. "We were so happy. That is a lot of money. I was able to take that money and invest it in my retirement savings plan. With some solid investments, I have been able to double that money since the time it was first invested."

Tom has been listening intently. He respects Walter for being smart with his money. In his head, it all sounds so simple. He thinks back to when he bought his house just a few years ago. He remembers his agent and all the document swapping she did.

"What about all those legal documents that need to be

filled out?" Tom inquires.

"That's where industry experts such as real estate lawyers come into play. You know, even when real estate agents are involved, third party services like this are necessary to complete transactions. These costs are always in addition to any commission rates charged by the agents.

"That's part of understanding the advantages of private sale. You still have access to the same professionals, without the commission of the agent. And that's one of the areas where PropertyGuys.com is a big help. They have contacts for these professionals here in town.

"And private selling is becoming more common. Did you know that one in four home sellers are deciding to sell privately? In the past, people wanting to sell without an agent had to settle for the orange and black 'For Sale by Owner' sign on the front yard. The private sale market has evolved to the point where private sale companies are now helping the home seller market their own homes on a national level as well. Now, for a one time, flat fee, home sellers can find marketing support and guidance when selling privately. These private sale companies bring credibility to those that want to sell privately."

The light bulbs begin to go on in Tom's head. While he's excited about what he's heard, he's still trying to piece it all together. "Walter, this sounds a lot like the time you booked all of our vacation tickets over the internet and saved us a pile of money. Is that what this is all about?"

"That's where it's all heading. The internet has become a change agent that is helping to eliminate the need for a middleman. As you recall, we were able to book our travel plans online without a travel agent. I invested the money I saved from my last home sale into my retirement plan and managed my account on the internet at a much lower commission rate than the traditional live broker. The internet is empowering people with information. I even looked for tips online as we were building your deck this past spring."

Walter smiles softly. "Real estate is no different. In fact, more people are going online to search for homes than ever before. The internet is cutting out the need for a real estate agent to market your home. And the potential savings are much greater.

"Remember how good it felt when we saved that money booking our vacation? Or when we bought the materials and built your deck? I think it's not just about savings, I think it's also about control."

2
The Critic

Tom heads home with his conversation with Walter fresh in his mind. His yard work will have to wait until later as he prepares to break the news to Julie about their neighbours leaving. It will be odd not having Walter and Carole around once they sell their house and move. Julie will find it strange also.

As Tom steps through his front door, he immediately begins calling for Julie to share the news with her. "Julie … Julie," Tom calls out in a raised voice.

"Shhh," Julie replies in an audible whisper. "Don't wake Billy. He's only been asleep for about half an hour. He could use another hour or so of rest."

Julie is in their living room on the main level, cuddled up in the corner of their sofa couch, reading 'What to Expect When You're Expecting'. She loved the book when she read it prior to her first child and thought it would be a fun read with their second child on the way.

Tom hangs his coat on the corner coat rack and tones down his voice as he continues: "Have you seen what's on the Williams' front lawn? They just put it up this morning."

Tom climbs the half-dozen steps and proceeds into the living room where Julie is sitting.

"No, I hadn't noticed," Julie replies. "What's there?"

Julie grabs the bookmark she had set on the coffee table and flags the page where she's ended up. She sets her book down and lifts herself off the couch. She meets Tom at the front window to take a peek at the target of their conversation. Tom continues, “Walter and Carole have put their house up for sale. I just got back from talking with Walter.”

The ‘For Sale’ sign catches Julie by surprise; she reacts much the same way Tom had when he first saw it.

While Tom and Walter have worked on a number of household projects together, Julie and Carole have also built a nice friendship. Carole will often watch little Billy if Julie has an errand or two to run during the day. Carole just loves watching their son. And she has so many toys left at home from when her kids were young. Billy really likes to look through all the old story books. For whatever reason, those are his favorites.

“Wow, I can’t believe it,” Julie says as she moves her head side to side to try and get the best view of the sign. “Well, we’ll certainly miss them once they leave.”

Julie can’t get a good look at the sign because one of the Williams’ well groomed evergreen trees is obstructing her view. “Who are they selling their house with?” Julie asks.

Julie’s curious to find out what real estate agent Walter is using. Her cousin, Sam Babbit, just got his real estate license a couple of months earlier. He had been talking about becoming a real estate agent ever since he lost his last job and wasn’t able to find other work. He finally decided to take the course towards the end of summer once some of his job leads had dried up.

Since he’s received his license, he practices his sales pitch on Julie all the time. He even wanted to list Tom and Julie’s house for fun. He thought that by listing their house, it might impress his broker because he was able to get a listing so quickly after the course.

Julie likes Sam and is always on the lookout for new homes for sale around the city. She takes note of the different real estate agents in town when she’s out doing errands; sort of sizing up the competition for Sam. There are a lot of agents in town. And they all want their hands on any available listing. Sam has already noticed how cut-throat the profession can be.

Sam has talked to Julie about helping him gather a client list so he can build his business. Now with the listing of her neighbour's house, she wonders if there is any opportunity for Sam to get involved in that sale.

"Walter's not using a real estate agent," Tom replies with confidence, having just spoken with him about the benefits of selling privately. "He's going to sell his home privately; and it sounds like he can save a lot of money doing it."

This puzzles Julie. She's always thought highly of the decisions Walter and Carole have made in the past, but this idea of selling privately didn't match up with what she understood to be a smart real estate move. Her cousin Sam needed to take a course to become a real estate agent so he could sell homes. All the conversations she has had with Sam indicated that an agent is extremely important to the home selling process.

"How are they saving money?" Julie asks, trying to figure out why someone wouldn't want to use an agent. "Sam always says that it's really the buyer that is paying the commission through the price of the home once it sells; it really doesn't cost the seller anything. It seems weird that they wouldn't want to take advantage of the free real estate agent services."

"Walter did say that they had tried using an agent before, when they sold their last house, but that it hadn't worked out," Tom replied, as he tried to put himself in Walter's shoes to come up with a smart answer. "I guess any time you have to write a check for 5 or 6% of the price of a home, it feels like you're the one paying the fee since it is coming out of your account."

"How come it didn't work out? They did end up selling

their home didn't they?" Julie wondered. "Are you saying they didn't use an agent?"

"Well, that's really what I found out in our conversation," Tom began. "Walter started with an agent, but after a few months, they decided to part ways, and Walter went about selling privately. Once Walter put the 'For Sale by Owner' sign up, he was able to control the price of the house, the appointments and the showings.

"Walter also told me that toward the end, his agent had asked him to lower his price. That was one of the reasons he decided to sell on his own. Between lowering the price and paying the commission, he wasn't going to have enough money left to be able to upgrade the way he and Carole had planned; there just wasn't going to be enough money anymore.

"Walter recognized that by selling on his own, there would be no commission to pay. By removing the real estate agent from the process, he was cutting out the major expense in selling a home. He knew he could do it himself."

"Maybe they just didn't have the right agent. Not all agents are the same. Maybe they should have tried another agent instead. I still don't know why you wouldn't want to use one," Julie replied, as she made her way back to the corner of the couch. "Sam learned in his real estate course that agents can sell a home faster and for more money; that they can take advantage of their network of buyers and sellers to make deals happen. Maybe their agent just didn't have the right connections."

"Maybe you're right. I suppose they could have tried another agent, but they did end up selling it on their own in the end." Tom walks over and plunks himself down in the arm chair next to the couch. "But that's an interesting question about getting more money.

"If you look at Walter's situation though, he did say he ended his contract with his agent because he asked him to lower his price. And, he was listed with that agent for a few months before they parted ways. It doesn't sound like his agent was able to sell his home or get him any more money. And he was using an experienced agent."

Julie feels the need to stick up for Sam and defend his profession. While she is not getting overly worked up about the conversation, she is beginning to ask the questions with a slightly aggrieved tone in her voice.

"So, who would have done the home showings for him once he decided to sell privately? Would Walter have had to do this himself?" Julie responds, as she tries to find ways to poke holes in the argument for selling privately.

"Home showings would seem to be a benefit of using an agent. I can see them being a hassle. Let someone else take care of that," Julie submitted. "Would you want to have to show your own home? I'm sure he would have had to spend a lot of time doing them."

"Yeah, Walter did his own showings but he never really mentioned how much time he spent doing them," Tom replies as he thinks back to his earlier conversation.

"He did say that he clearly knew his home better than any agent ever could. He said that agents aren't as familiar with the house as the owner is; this is especially true of buying agents. Most of the time when buying agents take clients through a house, it's their first time seeing it as well."

Tom could tell that Julie wasn't quite as open as he had been toward the whole private sale idea. Despite the answers to some of her questions, he could sense that she really wasn't willing to think about life without real estate agents. And he was realizing that Sam was the primary reason for her persistent position. Asking all these questions about Walter selling privately was Julie's way of sticking up for Sam and his profession.

"I bet it was a lot of time. Sam says that it's a lot of work. Part of an agent's full-time job is to provide these types of services. With Walter working the hours he does, I don't know why he would want to take on this extra burden. I wouldn't want to have to do an open house every Sunday until my house sold."

The every Sunday comment struck a chord with Tom. That is football day. Tom enjoys nothing more than to kick back in his favorite chair and watch an afternoon full of football games. He slumps down in his chair a bit as his mind drifts off for a moment, back to last week's gridiron action. A couple of his sports buddies had dropped by with some cold drinks; and the pizza they ordered was fantastic. His thoughts get interrupted by another question from Julie.

"And what if someone is interested? Where do the forms come from? How is a private seller protected? Real estate agents have all the proper legal forms to fill out to protect everyone in the process. Remember all the paper work we had to sign with the agent when we bought this house?" Julie continued. "Who would take care of that?"

"Well, you would still need a lawyer no matter how you decided to sell your home. Remember when we bought this house? In the end, the legal papers were exchanged between our lawyer and the seller's lawyer. And that would've been an additional cost to the seller; above and beyond the commission they had to pay." Tom responded, "And Walter did say that he worked with his own lawyer to make sure everything was in order. Selling privately, I guess the agent gets eliminated in favor of going directly to the lawyer."

"I guess the biggest flaw I see in selling privately is not getting your property on the multiple listing service that real estate agents provide. If you don't get your house listed there, then you will not be able to sell it. Everyone talks about the multiple listing service and how important it is when you're selling your house."

"That's a good point, Julie. I do hear people talk about

the multiple listing service when buying and selling homes," Tom conceded. "And I'm not sure where Walter's buyer came from last time. But you are right, having a place where people can find your home would be important to getting it sold. I do know that this time he is using a company called PropertyGuys.com to get his home listed on the internet."

"Sam's mentioned to me before about people that want to sell their own home," Julie responds. "He says that they are a great way for him to find potential listings since most of them end up giving up after a couple of weeks and going with a real estate agent. He doesn't know why anyone would want to bother with the headache in the first place. There is quite a bit to selling a home. Legal documents, showings, negotiating, closing, the lawyer, and that's why there are agents around. People need a professional to help them sell their house. If it was really that simple that anyone could do it, agents probably wouldn't need to take a course to get their real estate license."

"Does Walter have his license?" asks Julie.

"I don't think he needs one to sell his own home," Tom responds. "But I'm not sure. To be honest, before I spoke to Walter earlier, I really never thought much about how a house gets sold outside of using an agent. Walter seemed to raise a lot of interesting ideas when he said he was selling privately."

Julie seemed to raise a couple of good points also. It's obvious the basis of her doubt has a foundation in all the conversations she's had with Sam since he's become licensed. From these dialogues, Julie has come to believe that agents are a necessity to the real estate selling process. It's clear that Julie is not quite as receptive to the idea of "do-it-yourself" real estate.

At the same time, Tom's conversation with Walter really made him think about what he would do the next time he wanted to sell. And knowing that they would probably end up moving during the next couple of years as his family grew larger, it nonetheless seemed to hit home immediately for some reason — probably because of the savings.

Tom can't stop thinking about how much money Walter saved the first time he sold; and how he's going to save even more than that this time. He's not jealous of Walter, just impressed. With all this on his mind, he had wanted at least to get some of his thoughts out to Julie to see where she might stand on the subject. He has clearly found out.

Tom decides to let the conversation die down. He's going to head out the back door again to do the yard work he had intended on doing earlier in the day. Tom starts to get up out of his chair.

"Anyway honey, I should go out back and rake the leaves. I had started to do this earlier when I saw Walter in his yard. That's how I found out about the Williams selling their home," Tom finishes.

Realizing that Walter and Carole are still not tied to an agent, Julie thinks it might be a good idea for Tom to at least try and get a referral for Sam. Julie gets up from the couch and walks out to the kitchen and grabs one of Sam's business cards off the kitchen refrigerator. As Tom moves toward the sliding doors in the kitchen, she hands him the card in case he runs into Walter again that day. "Why don't you give Walter one of Sam's business cards in case he changes his mind? It would help both Walter and Sam."

"I guess I can mention this to Walter next time I see him," Tom says. He reluctantly agrees that he should at least mention Sam's name to Walter in case he needs an agent. Walter seemed pretty set on private sale, but Tom will run it by him the next time he sees him. "I'm going to finish up the yard work, I should be in shortly."

Tom is glad he doesn't have to make a selling decision today. While he's intrigued by the control and savings of selling privately, he definitely knows where his wife currently stands on the issue. It's clear he'd have some work to do to convince Julie of the benefits of private sale. When he gets around to mentioning Sam to Walter, he has a few more real estate questions he needs answered.

3
The Clarification

It's been a couple of days since Tom and Julie learned that their neighbours have put their house up for sale. The two of them are home getting ready to sit down for supper when the phone rings for Tom. It's Walter.

"Hi Tom, how are you doing tonight?" Walter begins.

"I'm doing great, Walter. How are things with you?" Tom replies.

"Just fine. Listen, I'm wondering if you are free tonight. I'm moving some things from the house and could use a couple of extra hands if you're available. If not, I can probably find someone else to help, but I didn't think you would mind if you aren't busy? It should only take a couple of hours," Walter asks politely. He has such a warm demeanor.

"Moving things? Have you sold your home already?" Tom asks surprised.

"No, not yet," Walter replies with a chuckle, "We're just getting ready for when we start the showings. We want to tidy up a bit, keep things simple for potential buyers when they come to see the house."

This is the first time Tom's heard of such a thing. He realized that you should always make sure the kids toys are put away and the animals are not around, but moving things before the sale? He'll need to find out more about this.

"That's interesting," Tom replies. "I don't think there

is anything going on over here tonight. I'd be glad to drop by and give you a hand. You'll have to tell me about this moving before the sale thing."

"No problem," Walter replies with a grin in his voice. "I'll see you around seven?"

"Seven it is," Tom replies. "We'll see you then."

Tom hangs up the phone just as Julie walks back in the kitchen. She had chased Billy into the other room as he was running away from his high chair. It's funny, sometimes Billy loves getting into the high chair and eating, while other times he wants nothing to do with it.

"What's on Walter's mind tonight?" Julie inquires.

"He wants me to go over and help him move some things from his house. He says he is getting the house ready for when buyers want to go through it." Tom responds, with a hint of curiosity. "I'm not sure what that's all about, but I said I'd drop by to help him around seven."

"Oh, don't forget to take one of Sam's business cards with you." She grabs another card off the refrigerator and hands it to Tom, assuming he's misplaced the one she gave him the other day. "If Walter ends up going with a real estate agent, Sam wouldn't be very impressed with me if I hadn't tried to get him some business."

Tom takes the card from Julie and puts it in his pocket. He's still not real crazy about talking to Walter about Sam and trying to drum up business for him. But since he told Julie he'd mention Sam's name to Walter, he'll have to make an effort. It could at least be a way to ask Walter more questions about private sale.

Tom, Julie and Billy finish eating. Tom excuses himself from the table and heads to their room to change into some work clothes before going over to Walter's. He remembers to take Sam's card out of his pocket and transfers it to his work pants. As he rushes past the kitchen, he says goodbye to Julie and Billy.

Tom grabs his jacket and work gloves on the way out

the door. No sooner than he steps outside, he sees the lights on in his neighbour's garage. Walter has already begun organizing the boxes that they will be loading onto the truck.

"Howdy neighbour," Tom exclaims as he walks past the cube van and into Walter's garage. "I see you've got a head start on me."

"Just trying to get a few things organized to make this go smoother," Walter replies as he writes a few item descriptions on the top of a box. There seems to be a dozen or so cardboard boxes and a number of pieces of furniture from various rooms in his house set to get loaded on the back of the truck.

"So why in the world are you moving things before you even sell the house. I've never even heard of that before. Where are you putting all this stuff?"

"Well, they actually have a fancy name for moving things before showing your house; it's called home staging." Walter responds in his educational tone. "I came across this idea one night as I was clicking through the television channels when I couldn't find anything to watch. I just happened to stop at this channel because of a commercial I liked when the next show that came on had people moving their belongings out of a house and onto the front lawn. I wasn't sure what the show was about at first, but I thought I would keep watching for a minute as there was nothing else on."

"One of the hosts of the show was talking about home staging and getting the house ready to show. At the time, it was a new term for me as well and I just watched the rest of the show out of curiosity. Then, knowing I was going to put my house up for sale, I started to do some research on the internet about home staging. I found a number of home staging websites that further explained what it's all about."

"That's interesting. So home staging means moving things out of your house before selling it?" Tom repeated, with a clear question in his voice.

"Well, moving things out of your house can definitely be a large part of home staging. But home staging is more than just moving stuff. It's about preparing your home for the showing. It could involve anything from painting rooms, moving furniture, removing furniture, redecorating, adding pictures, you name it. Really, home staging would involve anything that would enhance your home and make it more appealing or attractive to buyers."

"Many times, sellers have a lot of useless stuff around the house that, to a stranger, would just look like clutter. By cleaning up, or removing these pieces, it makes the house more presentable, and less biased towards the decorating tastes of the seller."

"We're going to put this stuff in my son's garage until we need it again. Hopefully, it won't take too long to sell our house and we will get all our belongings out of his garage and into our new place without too much inconvenience to him."

"Home staging seems like a great idea," Tom replies. "I knew that you should always clean up your house before people arrive, but I've never thought of taking it to that level, to actually remove clutter from the house. How do you know what should stay and what should go?"

"Well, in our situation, we simply try to use a little common sense. One of the terms I remember seeing on a website is 'depersonalization'. You don't want any potential buyers to get caught up by any of your personal preferences. You want them to only concentrate on the house. Not necessarily what's in the house."

"We look at the different rooms and decide what needs to stay, and what could be removed. There is a fine line between home staging and emptying out the house. But you know, there are companies that do specialize in helping home sellers stage their homes. They even go so far as renting out furnishings for your house; pictures, tables, lamps, etc: anything they can do to enhance the house and try and raise its value. It's incredible how space and décor can influence how people view your home."

Walter waves Tom toward the first heavy piece they will be loading onto the truck. It's an old bookshelf that they had in the hallway downstairs. Walter's packed all the books into a few boxes and now it's time to store this family treasure.

"Take this bookshelf for instance," Walter continues. "While Carole and I like having this in the downstairs hallway, it really makes the hallway look small. By removing it for showings, the hallway is opened up to give it a roomier feel; like it's a wide corridor between the rooms. We've just tried to do a few simple things to open up the house and make it look bigger."

"So home staging is all about getting the inside of your home in showroom condition," Tom states as if he's recapping their home staging conversation.

"You're mostly right. But don't forget about the outside of the house. Just to be clear, getting your house in showroom condition refers to both the interior and the exterior of the house. I've gone through houses in the past where the rooms were all neat and tidy, but when we got to the garage, we could see that they used it as the storage location for all their junk; we could hardly get through the garage door — things were strewn all over the place. It was uncomfortable to look at and put questions in our mind about the previous owners.

"That's why we're storing some things off our property. Not only do we want to make sure the inside of the house looks nice, but we also want the garage to be presentable as well. And don't forget the lawn, flower beds, shrubs and driveway. It's a complete package potential buyers will be looking at."

Tom's impressed. Once again, Walter has made this all sound so simple. As they begin to move the bookshelf across the garage and into the van, more questions cross Tom's mind. "Wow, you seem to have done a lot of research on home staging. Any other big home selling secrets you can share with me?"

"Well, Tom, there are really three keys to selling a home. First, your house must be in showroom condition. Second, you have got to ask a fair price. And third, your home must be exposed to as many people as possible," Walter replies.

They push the bookshelf up into the van, slide it to the front and proceed to the next piece of furniture. "Well, I might as well ask you about price since you're stuck with me while we load this truck," Tom says with a grin.

"I talked to the PropertyGuys.com rep about this also. As a private seller, there are really a couple approaches to setting a price for your home. Before choosing an approach however, you must be set on the motive."

"Isn't the motive to sell your home? That one seems pretty clear," Tom interjects.

"You would think it was that simple, but there are really two ways to price. You can either speculate on the market by pricing your house a little bit higher than you think you might get for it, or you can price it slightly lower which will often result in a quicker sale. Now, pricing to sell doesn't mean under pricing either, it means pricing based on what the market can bear."

"I guess determining motive wasn't that simple," Tom laughs.

"Once you know your pricing motive, you can then determine your approach. First, you can look around you. See what other houses are for sale in your neighbourhood. Compare the type and size of these houses to yours. Often there are very similar houses on the market that would give you a good idea of what yours might be worth. This approach is somewhat subjective from the seller's point of view, but it often provides a very good starting point to setting a price," Walter says.

"Second, you can always use the services of a professional appraisal company. For a few hundred dollars, you can have an industry expert come in and provide you with a professional view as to the value of your home. Again, this can be used as an exact figure, or it could be used as a starting point to set your price. You could either raise the price a bit to speculate, or lower it a bit for a quicker sale. PropertyGuys.com has contacts in this area also.

"Really, the value of pricing your home can't be underestimated. You could have lots of people seeing your home and it could be the neatest and tidiest place in the world, but if it is priced too high, people will stay away. There has to be appropriate value for the buyer.

"I have my home listed with PropertyGuys.com. People can see pictures and virtual tours of my house. But if my house is not priced right, people won't call. That's how important pricing is to selling."

"You want to hear something funny?" Walter continues with a bit of a chuckle.

"Sure," Tom replies.

"I've been doing some home searches on the internet over the past couple of months to see what the real estate market is like; both what's available and what the prices are like. I'll go to both private sale websites and real estate agent websites."

"From time to time, I will see a private sale listing switch from the private sale website to an agent website. And you know what the first thing that seller will do once they make the switch? They will lower their price. Now, whether they are doing that on their own, or the agent is asking them to do it, I'm not sure. But the lesson is the same.

"Why wouldn't you lower your price and continue to sell privately? Now, that poor seller will essentially take a double hit on the money that is going into their pocket.

They are going to get less money on the sale because they lowered their price, and then they are going to have to pay expensive commissions once the house does sell. Not a financially smart move."

"So how did you end up pricing your home?" Tom asks Walter.

"Well, since I've had my eye on the market for quite some time, I felt fairly comfortable setting my own price based on the other listings I've seen," Walter replies. "I know what I paid for the house when I bought it and I have a good idea about the market. So I set my own price based on some comparable properties I've seen."

"But I also think using an appraiser is a smart decision as well. For those home sellers that are really not sure what their house is worth, they could hurt themselves by pricing their home too low. Again, for a few hundred dollars, these home sellers could be sure that they've priced their home properly by using an appraiser."

Again, Tom is amazed by how simple this whole thing sounds. He does have a question relating to agents and price; something he overheard Sam tell Julie back when he was trying to list their house after he received his real estate license.

"Julie's cousin, Sam Babbitt, is a real estate agent. He just started in the business a couple of months ago. Anyway, can't real estate agents set price as well? I think they do a market analysis or something like that?" Tom asks Walter.

"Yes, they can help as well. They take a look at similar homes for sale on the market as well as homes that have sold in that area over a certain period of time. They use their multiple listing service data to review historic sales and compare them with existing houses on the market to help come up with a price. It's essentially the same as what you or I could do with comparing to current homes for sale, except they have access to historical sales data through their system."

Walter continues to share his thoughts on this agent service. "The question becomes, what would be more accurate? Using price comparisons of homes that are currently on the market to come up with a value for your home or prices of homes that have sold in the past? I believe that current home prices are more accurate; and we have access to that information on the internet. While the agent system may have more results to compare to than you or I do, is it really more accurate and is it worth the commission that's paid?"

Tom is taking this all in. The more Walter talks about private sale, the more interested he becomes. While he knows he won't be selling right away, he does want to learn all he can. He knows he'll need to have it all figured out if he's ever to convince Julie that it's a smart way to sell.

"Okay, so now I know the price I want to ask for my house, and it's in showroom condition, how do I make sure as many people as possible get to see my house when I sell it privately?" Tom asks inquisitively.

"Exposing your home can be done any number of ways." Walter begins "Today, most people that try to sell on their own will use some type of private sale system to help them market their home. In my opinion, PropertyGuys.com is the best one out there. They are a national company and have a wide range of tools. They provide a professional 'For Sale' sign, a web listing, still pictures, virtual tours, automated telephone messages, feature sheets, newspaper classified ads, supporting documents and other materials. Although I've only been listed with them for a few days, I've been really pleased with the service.

"What about open houses? Are they a good idea?" Tom asks. Knowing that agents use open houses, Tom assumes that this is a valuable tool to sell a home.

"It's funny you should mention them," Walter replies,

"When selling privately, they are really not all that important. An individual showing is much more valuable because you have a set time that you know someone is coming to take a look at the house."

"Open houses are seen by many as a way that real estate agents, the selling agent, can build their client list. You see, when selling agents hold open houses, the visitors are typically buyers that are not accompanied by another agent. These potential buyers, which are often home sellers as well, become good prospects for the agent holding the open house. The selling agent really has two motivations to hold an open house; show the house and increase their client list."

"These days, a good web listing that provides enough detail and pictures of a house, is a great introduction to a house for serious shoppers. These listings can be considered 24/7 virtual open houses, where interested buyers can then contact the owner if there is some serious interest in the listing. The key is to select a company that gets a lot of buyers visiting their website to make sure your property will be seen.

"Take PropertyGuys.com for instance. They get a lot of website traffic; millions of hits a month. My listing has both pictures and a virtual tour of my house. It also has all the information about my house on there. People get a real good feel for the house when they visit the website. People that see it and are interested by what they see will get in touch and set up an appointment to come see it.

"What's nice about PropertyGuys.com is that I can tell exactly how many times my house gets seen. They keep a count of the number of times my listing is displayed."

Tom remembered that Julie was curious as to who did Walter's showings on the last home he sold. She also mentioned that it must have been time consuming. This seems like a good time for Tom to ask Walter about that.

"Did you handle your own showings when you sold

your last home? How long did they take?" Tom asks.

"Yeah, I did them myself. Really, they didn't take that long at all. When a potential buyer calls, you set up a time with them that they can stop by and visit. Typically, a first run through of the house will take fifteen or twenty minutes and then you ask them if they have any further questions.

"The nice thing is that since you are booking your own showings, you can pick times that fit within your schedule. Plus, with my information on the website, you're really only going to show the home to people that are really interested. This also cuts down on wasted time and reduces the number of 'tire-kickers'."

"Tire-kickers?" Tom interjects. This is a new term for him.

"Yeah, the type of person who just wants to see what the inside looks like without any real intention of buying. They could be interested in anything from layout, to design, to backyard size, anything but buying. Detailed listings on the internet really help reduce these types of inquiries as they can get their fix on the website." Walter says grinning.

"Well, isn't that what the agents' multiple listing service is all about? Wouldn't you want to be on there?" Tom wonders aloud.

"Sure, the multiple listing service is the agent's main source for all of the listings represented by agents. With PropertyGuys.com, they provide much more information, with a lot better visual options. For example, many agent listings don't provide addresses online, or virtual tours. PropertyGuys.com come in and take the pictures and the virtual tours for you. Then they put all of your information online – including address and contact information.

"The PropertyGuys.com representative said she would come back after we finish staging our home, and take some more photos and virtual tours for me. She is a great help."

"But won't you lose out on buyers that use agents?" Tom asks. "If you are selling privately, and not dealing with an agent, then won't you miss out on those buyers that do use agents?"

"That's a good question because you would naturally think that's the case," Walter responds, acknowledging the logic behind the question. "When I was doing research on selling privately, one of the interesting statistics that I came across was that almost four out of every five buyers start looking for homes on the internet before they make a call to a real estate agent.

"And when you stop and think about it, there is some logic behind this changing behavior on the part of home buyers," Walter continues. " Remember how we talked the other day about the internet changing the way people book travel or buy stocks. Because all the information required to make a decision can be found on the internet, people can now do these things themselves.

"Well, the same is now starting to apply to real estate. Before the internet, the real estate agent was important to buying a home because they were the ones that controlled all the information about what homes were for sale. You needed to work with an agent to get access to this information.

"Now all that information is easily accessible on the internet. And it's searchable. I don't need a buying agent to see what homes are available for sale. I can simply go online and look around.

"And it's this same shift in mindset that has allowed private sale companies to grow in popularity. While the online multiple listing service is an important tool for real estate agents to market homes, it can cost 5% or more in sales commissions for home owners to get their properties listed there through real estate agents.

"Private sale companies make it easier for people that want to sell their own home to take advantage of this same type of exposure on the internet. And like I said before, they usually provide more detailed information."

"But what about buyers that already have an agent," Tom asks. "Can they still buy from someone selling privately?"

"Sure they can," Walter responds, "Selling privately essentially means that you have chosen not to deal with a selling agent; that you are marketing, showing and negotiating the house yourself. Buyers' agents can still bring their clients by to view a private sale house.

"In this type of situation, what often happens is the buyer agent will negotiate a commission with either the buyer or the seller. This commission rate is typically somewhere around half the normal commission rate (2-2.5%) since only one agent is getting paid. As you may know, in a traditional real estate sale, where there is a buying agent and a selling agent, the negotiated commission rate, usually somewhere around 5% or 6%, the commission is split between the buying agent and the selling agent.

"Years ago, selling privately was much more challenging. Before the internet took off, the only option that existed for people who wanted to sell on their own was the orange and black 'For Sale by Owner' signs that they could buy at their local department store. Outside of providing a phone number on the sign, there was really no way to provide the type of information a good website listing can provide – address, home details, photos, virtual tours, that type of stuff.

"Today, buyers can really get a good feel for a house over the internet if the listing has detailed information, lots of pictures and a virtual tour. This helps them narrow the homes they want to visit to the ones they are really interested in.

"If you noticed, that is why I don't have the old black and orange 'For Sale by Owner' sign on my front lawn. I went with PropertyGuys.com because they specialize in marketing people's homes.

"But you still have to be careful which private sale company you list with. There are a number of companies that promote themselves as 'For Sale by Owner' companies – or FSBO (pronounced Fisbo) companies – that simply allow you to upload a photo and a few details online. They typically offer very little support after the fact. You're probably not going to get the best bang for your dollar at these minimal service sites.

"PropertyGuys.com is a national company that provides marketing and support for the listing. I didn't want just a local company as buyers can ultimately come from all over. I set an appointment with their representative and she came to the house to install the sign, take the pictures for the still photos. She's coming back to take updated still photos and virtual tour photos once I get these boxes out of here. She also left behind some legal documents that can be used in negotiation and to send to the lawyer. She went back to her office and uploaded the information online and added a voice recording of my property for their automated phone feature. The company offers additional print services like weekly classified ads if I wanted them.

"People are always looking on the internet for real estate. PropertyGuys.com specializes in getting these buyers to end up on its website through the use of search engines like Google and Yahoo!, driving potential buyers to my listing. Once the buyers are there, they offer multiple search options such as ID number, city selection and map drill downs. PropertyGuys.com also offers tools such as automated emails and 'send to a friend' that will help get my property in front of people.

Tom inserts: "Did I hear you say they provided you with legal documents?"

"Yes, they provide you with legal templates to fill out," Walter responds to Tom's latest question. "The documents guide you through what information is needed for a lawyer to close the transaction. These forms come in handy when you are sitting across from a serious buyer and you get to the point of receiving an offer."

"These templates can then be taken to a lawyer to have them legally drawn up. One word of caution though: some companies will provide actual legal documents, so if both parties end up signing them, it could be considered an actual binding agreement. The safe bet would be to fill the documents out and get the lawyer to review before getting the signatures on them.

"What's nice about PropertyGuys.com is that they have local legal partners that will help you with any questions you might have; kind of a legal guide through the sale. They can handle the drawing up of the final agreements, any required updates to these documents and the closing. And these partners are obviously familiar with selling privately, which makes the whole process that much easier.

"Wow, so there is really a whole market being built around people who want to sell their own home," Tom states, captivated by all the knowledge Walter has accumulated on the subject.

"And you don't need a real estate license to do all this?" Tom asks again, just to make sure he's clear on what Walter is saying.

"Not at all. More people are starting to look at private sale as a way to stay in control of the sale and save money," Walter replies.

"But are people really saving money by selling privately?" Tom inquires. "Julie's cousin Sam always says that it's really the buyer that is paying the commission through the price of the home. If this is true, then aren't real estate agent services essentially free and all the work required by a private seller to show and negotiate the home unnecessary when the services are available for nothing?"

"Let's face it. Real estate markets sell homes, not

necessarily real estate agents. It's all about supply and demand. Agents really coordinate the sale of homes. With the right marketing approach, a properly priced home will get attention from potential buyers whether or not an agent is involved.

"And if we look at it from the perspective that similarly featured homes will ultimately sell for similar prices, regardless of whether an agent is involved or not, then the cost of the commission really becomes an expense to the seller; not a surplus gift from the buyer."

"Not only is the commission an expense, but people are also recognizing that the traditional commission structure is outdated and flawed. Let's say I'm selling my house for $200,000 and you are selling yours for $250,000. We use the same agent and get essentially the same services. At a 6% commission rate, I would pay the agent $12,000 plus taxes and you would pay $15,000 plus taxes. Does this make any sense to you? Remember, we are essentially getting the same service, but not paying nearly the same price for it."

"I've never thought of it that way. It does seem odd," Tom admits. "So are you saying that real estate agents aren't really necessary to the whole process? I can't imagine that they are too happy about that."

"In a way, yes," Walter replies, picking his words carefully, "But I would never say that private sale will run real estate agents out of town completely. Agents do have value for some sellers, just like stock brokers have value for some investors and travel agents have value for some travelers."

"You see, there will always be some people due to circumstances that won't be able to sell their own home; they may have been transferred and are no longer in town, they may be elderly and worried about security, they may simply be uncomfortable showing or negotiating on their own, or there may be some other reason. For these people, agents may be worth the cost for them."

"However, more and more people are recognizing that there are enough tools and support, that the 'do-it-yourself', self-starter type person can be comfortable in selling their own home and saving a considerable amount of money by doing so."

"Really Tom, the question is not whether a real estate agent can sell a home, but whether or not a home owner can sell their own home. If the answer is yes, then there are considerable cost savings that one can realize."

Tom and Walter have been working diligently throughout their conversation. They've almost got the cube van completely packed with the boxes and furniture that were sitting out in Walter's garage. As they load the last box on the back of the trailer, Walter pulls down the sliding door, latches and locks it shut, and reaches out for Tom's hand.

"Thanks a million for your help tonight Tom," Walter says genuinely.

"No problem at all. I always enjoy spending time over here. I'll definitely miss that once you guys leave."

"Me too," Walter interjects.

"But I've got to get going now," Tom continues. "Julie has a doctor's appointment in the morning. She's going to her first ultrasound for this pregnancy. I've got to get up early, get Billy ready and take him to daycare in the morning. Julie's excited to see the baby for the first time."

"Well, tell her we said hi and we hope all goes well!" Walter exclaims.

"Will do," Tom says "I'm sure we'll be talking soon."

"Oh, by the way," Tom continues as he reaches into his pocket and pulls out Sam Babbitt's business card, the one Julie had given to him earlier. He hands it to Walter as he smiles coyly, "Julie gave me this card. It's her cousin Sam Babbitt; he's a real estate agent. Anyway, she wanted me to give it to you. I know you probably won't need it, but I've got to be able to tell her I gave it to you; you know what I mean."

"Thanks, Tom," Walter replies. "I'm pretty sure I'll be fine on my own. But tell Julie I appreciate her help."

"I'll let her know." Tom says as he turns to go home. "We'll be in touch soon."

4
The Crisis

Tom walks back in his office and checks his voice messages. It's been quite a morning. Julie had the ultrasound appointment to attend, so he had to take care of Billy, get him dressed, fed and off to daycare. Julie usually takes care of that. Her job is a little more flexible and she doesn't start as early as Tom does, which allows her to get Billy to daycare at a reasonable time each morning. Each time Tom takes a turn in getting Billy ready, he realizes again just how much work it is.

Tom would have preferred to go to the ultrasound appointment with Julie. Unfortunately for him, the appointment was set for the same day as their quarterly meetings at work, a meeting that he knew he couldn't get out of because of its importance to the operation of his department. He had to give a presentation to the executive group on a new product he'd been researching.

Tom dials into his voice mail: two new messages. The first is from one of his suppliers. It sounds like the shipment was out the door on time and should arrive as expected. The second is from Julie. She sounds happy, excited and a little hesitant all at the same time.

"Hi Tom. It's me. I am just leaving the hospital with my mother and had to call you right away. Everything went fine at the ultrasound, but you've got to give me a call on my cell as soon as you get this message. Love you."

Tom has no idea what this could be. If the ultrasound went fine, did she run into someone in the hospital that he should know about? Was it a friend? A relative? He'll find out soon enough.

Since it's been a couple of hours since the message was left, he decides to call Julie at home. She decided to take the day off because of the ultrasound and was going to pick Billy up on her way home from the hospital. He figures she'd be there by now. He dials his home number and waits for a response on the other end.

"Hello," Julie answers.

"Hey honey, what's going on?" Tom says with a slight quickness in his voice, "I got your message. What's up?"

"Well, the ultrasound went well this morning. Everything looks great. Both babies are doing well ..."

"Both babies?" Tom interrupts in a surprised voice.

"Yep, both babies. We're having twins!" Julie exclaims.

"Get out of here. We're having twins?" Tom repeats in disbelief.

"I know. I couldn't believe it either. The technician was moving the ultrasound wand around trying to get the best view of the baby when she noticed something that looked like a second heartbeat. After a few minutes of trying to get a better look, she confirmed that there were indeed two babies."

"Incredible!" Tom exclaimed.

"But it may explain why I've been more tired and felt a little more nauseous than when I was pregnant with Billy. The technician was saying that often times pregnancy symptoms are multiplied when there is more than one baby in there."

Julie gets somewhat serious for a moment as she probes for Tom's honest opinion. "So, what do you think?"

"I think it's great. It's a little shocking and unexpected, but we can make it work. We may have to start looking for that larger house we always talked about," Tom replies.

Tom and Julie have always thought their current house was a good size for the three of them, and would be adequate with a second child until the two kids got a little older, or they decided to have a third. Now that the family is growing by two, they will have to seriously reconsider their living arrangements.

"We'll talk more about this when I get home tonight," Tom continues.

Tom and Julie finish their phone conversation and hang up. Tom starts thinking back to all the things he and Walter have talked about. Their conversations now have a sense of serendipity attached to them; like they were in preparation for an upcoming event of which Tom was unaware.

The afternoon goes by slowly for Tom. He is anxious to get home and see Julie and find out all the details of the ultrasound. Julie was supposed to get ultrasound photos to bring home and show Tom, but with all the excitement, he had forgotten to ask her about them on the phone. As the afternoon drew to an end, Tom decided to leave work a few minutes early to beat the rush and get home faster.

The drive home gave Tom some quiet time to think about all the changes that are about to come. Double everything; cribs, diapers, clothes, car seats, strollers, the list seemed to go on forever. And the house. Tom really thinks they'll need to start looking for a bigger place to live to accommodate their growing family.

Now Tom and Julie will need to determine how they're going to sell their house.

His private sale conversations begin to fill his mind. He'd love to be able to save thousands of dollars when they finally do sell. There are so many upcoming expenses now that they are having twins. He knows it will be an interesting conversation with Julie, but he'd really like to sell privately if they do in fact decide to sell.

Tom arrives home to the sight of his beautiful wife

waiting for him. She hears him drive in and is at the top of the stairs waiting for him to come in. In one hand, she is holding Billy's hand as he stands next to her, and in the other, she is holding the ultrasound pictures of their twins. She's beaming.

"Hi Tom," Julie greets Tom as he comes through the door.

"Hey everybody," Tom says grinning, acknowledging them both as they watch him take off his coat. "How's everyone doing?"

"Mommy having two babies," Billy blurts out as he points to his mom's belly. They both burst out laughing at the innocence in his eyes and the softness of his voice.

"Isn't that exciting, buddy?" Tom says to Billy as he picks him up in his arms. He leans over and gives his wife a gentle kiss.

"Did mommy show you the pictures of the two babies?" Tom lets his wife put the ultrasound pictures in front of them as she points out the contours of the two babies in the image.

What an exciting time. All three make their way to the couch and look over the ultrasound photos a few times as they talk about how their lives will change with twins. Billy quickly loses interests and heads to his room to find some toys. The conversation makes its way to the topic of the house.

"I've been doing a lot of thinking since we found out we were having twins. I know we've talked about eventually moving into a large house over the next few years, but I really think we need to start looking for a bigger place now. We need to find a house and get moved in before the twins arrive," Tom states.

Julie could tell he had given this some thought. And this didn't surprise her in the least. They had talked so frequently about upgrading, that they both knew it was just a matter of time. She figured that the news of the twins would cause them to start seriously thinking of moving.

"It's funny you say that," Julie replies. "I knew that you would want to move right away. My mom and I were talking about it on the drive home from the hospital."

"Speaking of moving, Sam's coming over tonight to talk about listing our house and giving us a free market analysis," Julie continued.

This caught Tom a little off guard. While he was prepared to get their house on the market right away, he and Julie really hadn't talked about what exactly they were going to do and when they were going to do it. And with all the things he's learned from Walter in the past few days, he's not really sure if he wants to list with an agent. He really wants to try and sell privately. But he doesn't want to jump to conclusions right away either. He's got to approach this delicately.

"Really, how come you called him already?" Tom asked. "It's pretty quick isn't it?"

"Well, I didn't call him. He called us. After we spoke earlier today, Sam called and congratulated us on the twins and asked me if we wanted him to come over and talk about listing our house. I figured we were going to talk to him eventually, so I said, 'Sure, come on by.'"

"How did Sam find out so quickly?" Tom asked curiously.

"Through my mom, I guess. On the way from the hospital today, we were talking about our growing family and I mentioned that we were probably going to need to move. After she had gotten home, she called her sister to tell her the news of the twins.

"Somehow, the fact that we were going to move came up and I guess my aunt called Sam once they got off the phone. You know how news spreads in my family," Julie says with a grin. "It's okay that he's coming over tonight, isn't it?"

"I guess so," Tom says with a slight hesitation.

"Did you want to wait?" Julie replies. "I thought we just decided we wanted to upgrade right away. Is there something you wanted to wait for?"

"No, not at all. I guess with all the conversations I've had with Walter, and the chance to save thousands of dollars in commission, I thought that might be a good way to go. You know, to try and sell privately." Tom replies in a soft voice, not really wanting to have the full blown discussion at the moment, but wanting to get his thoughts out in the open. "I guess we can wait and see what Sam has to say. We can talk more after that."

"I still don't think selling privately is as easy as Walter makes it sound," Julie replies, making her position clear. "I'm sure Sam will be able to convince you once he stops by tonight."

While Tom is not so sure, he leaves the conversation at that for the moment. This meeting with Sam should be interesting.

They decide to eat supper earlier than normal since Sam is coming by to talk about selling their house with them. As they finish cleaning up the kitchen, they hear the door bell ring. It sounds like Sam is here.

Julie walks down to the door and lets Sam in. As she greets him with a hello, she takes his coat and hangs it in the main floor closet at the top of the stairs. Sam removes his shoes and makes his way to the top of the stairs.

"Hey, Tom," Sam begins. "Quite the news today, wasn't it?"

"Sure was," Tom replies from the kitchen. "Can you believe it? Twins! I'm still trying to get used to the whole idea. But we are pretty excited about it."

"Can I get you something to drink?" Julie chimes in as they move toward the living room.

"No, I'm fine for now, I think." Sam replies.

Tom meets them in the living room as they all take a seat and talk for a moment about the pregnancy, twins, and how life is going to change having to raise two babies at once. This leads them perfectly into the reason why Sam has showed up: to talk about the sale of their house.

"So I heard from my mother, who was talking to yours, that you guys are probably looking at moving now that you'll have the extra little one crawling around. I figured you guys would probably need a hand with that, and that's why I called you earlier.

"I hope you don't mind, but I took the liberty of printing off a few home comparisons so that we could come up with a price for your home." Sam pulls out a stack of paper from his briefcase with a number of different homes on them and begins to share how he would price their home based on similar listings on the market.

Sam also pulls out a listing agreement from his local real estate board. "When exactly did you want to list your home?" Sam asks. "If you want to sign this agreement, I can get this up for you over the next day or so."

Wow, this is getting formal fast, Tom thinks to himself as Sam lays the document on the coffee table in front of them. Not two minutes in the door and Sam is already asking for them to sign a listing agreement.

While they do want to act quickly, Tom wants to put the brakes on this conversation; at least drop it down a gear. He's still not convinced he wants to sign with a real estate agent. While he likes Sam, he's not willing at this point to give up so much money in commissions when his home sells. He can't get the idea of a private sale out of his mind, and he knows if he were to sign that document now, he'd be uneasy about the decision. He feels he needs to mention this to Sam.

"To be honest, Sam, this is pretty new for us. While we know we want to upgrade to a bigger home, we still have a couple things we are trying to sort through before we actually put our home on the market. I'm not sure we want to make that commitment without a little bit more information," Tom interjects, trying in a roundabout way to broach the topic of private sale.

"Our neighbour Walter is selling his home privately and, after talking with him, there seems to me to be a lot of good reasons to do so. The main reason is the thousands of dollars we could save by not having to pay a commission. There are a lot of things we could do with that kind of money; we've got a lot of expenses coming up with the twins. We'll have to buy double everything."

"Actually, I noticed the sign on your neighbour's front lawn as I was driving by. I see he's listed with PropertyGuys.com; a private sale company. He had to pay an upfront fee to get listed with that company; probably a few hundred dollars. And there is no guarantee he will sell his home," Sam replies as he addresses Walter's decision to sell privately.

"But it's like I've always told Julie, it's really the buyer that is paying the commission. You don't have to pay a dime until the house sells and, once it does, the commission comes from the money you've received from the buyer," Sam continues, confident in his answer,

"That's what's nice about using an agent, we don't have to pay anything until the house sells," Julie says as she sides with Sam. "There are no upfront costs."

"That's true, Julie," Tom states as he turns toward his wife to address her point. "We wouldn't have to pay until the house sells, but we would be paying thousands and thousands of dollars more once it did."

"And I'm not sure I really agree that the buyer is paying the commission," he continues, turning back toward Sam. "When a home sells, it's the seller that writes the commission check to the agent. It's not the buyer. Commission checks are written from the proceeds of the sale, and it's an expense that a private seller would not have to worry about. It sounds like a cost to the seller to me."

Sam really wasn't prepared for a private sale debate.

He had come to the house expecting to get the listing since it was a family connection. He tries to answer this question the best he can.

"Buyers are paying because agents can get more money for a house," Sam states. "Because we have access to buyers and sellers, we can typically get a better price for you."

Tom thinks for a moment. This seems to fly contrary to the market situation he and Walter had talked about over the last week or so.

"If private sellers and real estate agents are both using market comparisons to set selling prices for homes, then how can an agent get more money for a house than someone that is selling privately? Aren't both essentially starting from the same point: market value?" Tom asks Sam.

"And with the number of people using the internet continuing to rise, aren't buyers going online and doing their own research before ever contacting a real estate agent? With a good website listing, won't private sellers also have access to these buyers?"

Sam sidesteps the question somewhat by providing a related answer to the question: "Well, let's face it, there is a cost to selling your home and for the services an agent provides. An agent will help you set a price, market your home, show it, decrease the number of unqualified buyers or 'tire-kickers', negotiate the sale, fill out the legal documents for you and help you at closing."

Tom pauses and repeats this list in his mind. There is really nothing on that list that he and Walter have not talked about. None of these things seem to be all that difficult or worth the cost of the commission.

"I do understand some of the things an agent does for the seller, but how does any of that get a seller more money. It sounds like you might be able to save sellers some time, but then the question for sellers becomes 'Is the time saved worth the commission spent?'"

"Well, I would argue that the services we provide are important," Sam replies. "Real estate agents have to take a course to make sure they have all the bases covered in a real estate transaction. People need a professional real estate agent to make sure things go smoothly. We add value for the home seller."

As Tom listens to Sam answer his probing questions about agent services, he notices that his answers become increasingly generic. That he is kind of resorting to industry jargon instead of straight facts. But Tom continues to listen for the one idea that would change his mind back to wanting to use a real estate agent.

"People who go to the local department store and buy a black and orange 'For Sale by Owner' sign aren't usually that successful," Sam returns to a subject that he feels he can defend. "Did you know that most of those people eventually sign up with a real estate agent? The signs are very unprofessional and its marketing potential is limited really to people that drive by."

"I would agree with you on that," Tom replies, happy that they can find some common ground in the discussion. "The old 'For Sale by Owner' method really leaves the home seller on his own to fend for himself. The black and orange signs have limited exposure and don't really do anything to promote the features of a house."

"But today there is a lot more support for selling privately. For example, our neighbour is using PropertyGuys.com. They'll come in and install a professional 'For Sale' sign, take photos for website listings, create virtual tours, provide all the property details including price, location and features, add automated voice messages of the property, offer directional arrows, legal documents and additional advertising through their print options. They're also around to provide overall support and answer any questions a home seller might have on selling a home. They have even developed partnerships with other industry professionals so that they can guide and direct the home seller through the different steps of selling privately."

"That's fine, but real estate agents have access to the multiple listing service. Isn't that where most people go to find a home these days?" Julie asks as she tries to help Sam build his case.

"I would agree that this is one place that they go to find homes; but it's not the only place anymore," Tom answers, "Private sale companies have spent a lot of time and resources directing potential buyers to their website where their client listings are posted. Walter told me that PropertyGuys.com is getting millions of hits a month and offer buyer services such as advanced searches, buyer emails, and 'email a friend' features. Selling privately is advancing quickly as more people learn about this option."

"I didn't realize that private selling was that organized," Julie admits. "I always thought it was just a sign on the front yard and that was it."

A lot of this is news to Julie. She is curious to know how much Sam knows about private sale. "Did you know about these companies, Sam?"

Tom picked up on Julie's surprise at just how organized the private sale market has become. He'll need to keep this in mind as they discuss private sale in the future.

"Yeah, I knew they existed," Sam responded. "But our association really hasn't been all that concerned with them so far. People will always need real estate agents they tell us; and I believe them."

Tom believes there is some truth to what Sam is saying. However, while some people may always need real estate agents, Tom wonders if as many people will need them. As people begin to learn about private sale, as Tom has, he believes there will be more individuals that will look at private sale as a real alternative to high commission costs.

The evening is beginning to fade away. Sam wants this listing. He's played along so far and tried to tread lightly as he answered each of Tom's questions. But now he recognizes its time to be blunt with them. He wants to get them to sign the agreement before he leaves.

"Look, I can tell you have thought about this for awhile. You're smart people. But I don't want you guys to waste your time trying to do this on your own, when I can help you sell your home. If you are serious about selling now, then you will want to list with a real estate agent and get your home on the multiple listing service.

"If you sign this document now, I can have you on the multiple listing service right away," Sam follows up, making sure he's explicit in what he's asking for.

"Why don't you give us a little time to think about it." Tom responds.

"You could wait, but I know our broker always has people looking for this type of home. Actually, they started a program recently that will guarantee that your house sells, or they will buy it from you," Sam says in response to Tom's request for time, "I can get you added to this program if you want."

"Are you sure you don't want to sign up now?" Sam asks a second time.

"That sounds like an interesting program," Julie says. "Tom, would something like that work for us?"

Tom recognizes that last sales pitch as one of the lines that Walter had warned him about.

"I think Julie and I are going to need to talk about some things before we commit to a listing. Maybe we should wrap it up for the night. It is getting kind of late," Tom replies, looking at Julie. "How about we get back to you by the end of next week?"

Sam agrees reluctantly. He's dying to get the listing and a little disappointed that they're even talking about private sale. But he bites his tongue because they are family.

The conversation quickly turns to the excitement of the day and the upcoming birth of twins. Sam hangs around for a minute or two before he makes his way towards the door. Tom and Julie wish him well and confirm that they will get back to him over the next week.

Nothing Tom has heard from Sam has come close to changing his mind. He just needs to figure out a way now to get Julie on his side.

"I don't know, Julie," Tom begins. "I can't help but think we could save thousands of dollars in commissions by selling privately. I am pretty confident I could do it. Walter and I have talked about all the things Sam mentioned tonight."

"Well, at this point, I think we should list with him," Julie shares her opinion. "After all, he is family you know."

"I know, Julie," Tom replies with conviction. "But I feel like we need to look after our family. Those thousands of dollars could help us a lot."

5
The Buyer

The next day, the sun rises to welcome a beautiful Saturday morning. As Tom and Julie often do, they venture out with Billy to the local farmers market for some fresh fruits and vegetables. It's become a nice way to start the weekend and spend some quality time together. They love the smells of the fresh food that fill the air. Billy always points to a little country bakery that has a stand in the smallest of corners where he likes to get a muffin. For whatever reason, he never seems to forget that it is there.

The family finishes their shopping and they all return back to their mid-size, four door sedan. Julie straps Billy into his car seat as Tom puts the grocery bags in the trunk. They take their places in the front seats and Tom begins to back out of their parking spot. As Tom turns toward the middle of the car, looking out the back window, he catches a glimpse of Billy's car seat and the small amount of space it leaves in the backseat.

"Do you realize that we'll probably need to get a new car now, too?" he says as he puts the car in drive and proceeds down the road. "We could have put one more car seat in the back with Billy's, but now we'll need two more. There's just no room for three children in this car."

Tom and Julie love their sedan. It is so good on gas. They had actually bought the four door vehicle with the intention of having a couple of children, but three is beyond the capacity of the little car. They will need to look for an alternative. Perhaps they'll be able to trade it in for some sort of mini-van or sport utility vehicle. Whatever they get, it will definitely need to have more room.

"That's true," Julie replies. "I never thought of that. I knew we'd need doubles of things like cribs and high chairs, but I never even thought about cars. We'll need to start looking for something that will accommodate three car seats. Billy is probably still going to need one for another few years."

"That's going to be a huge expense," Julie continues. "We're just at the end of paying this car off and now we'll have to get something new. Even by trading this in, it's going to cost us thousands of dollars to upgrade."

"And whatever we end up getting will definitely be harder on gas," Tom adds. "We're really going to have to sit down and figure out how we are going to make this work."

"The more we think about it, the more the twins are going to change our lives." Tom continues, pointing out the obvious. "I knew a second child would put a little pressure on us, but an extra two will put a lot of pressure on us; especially financially."

"Homes, cars, supplies ..." Tom interrupts himself. "Speaking of homes, we need to tell Walter and Carole about the twins."

"That's right," Julie agrees, "With all the people that called yesterday to wish us well, we never did get in touch with them."

Tom and Julie pull into their driveway. Julie opens the back door to get Billy out and take him inside. Tom unlocks the front door of the house and retreats back toward the car to get the groceries out of the trunk. As he approaches the trunk, he sees Walter out on his front step, waving to a couple leaving his house. Now would be a good time to go and tell Walter about the great news.

Tom puts the groceries inside the front door and yells to Julie that he's heading next door to talk to Walter. She agrees and he shuts the door behind him and proceeds to his neighbour's house.

"Hey Walter, how are things today?" Tom shouts over to Walter, as he makes his way towards his place. "Beautiful day isn't it?"

"It sure is." Walter replies with a grin. "How are things with you and Julie? How did her ultrasound go? I remember you saying the other night that she was to have it yesterday. Hope all went well."

"Let's just say it went too well, with the emphasis on TWO," Tom says wittily, "We're having twins."

"Twins?" Walter replies with clear surprise in his voice. "Well, good for you guys! That's pretty exciting. Double the fun!"

"Definitely gives us a lot to think about," Tom replies. "It's kind of ironic. Last week at this time we were shocked to hear you guys were moving. Now, we are going to have to consider moving also. Our place will be too small to have two more little ones running around."

"Life's funny sometimes, isn't it?" Walter chuckles. "Speaking of moving, did you see that couple that was leaving as you were pulling into your driveway?"

"Yes, I did." Tom replies.

"That couple was here to take a look the house," Walter said, "They were my second showing. I had one last night too."

"Really," Tom says with a hint of excitement "How did it go today?"

"I think it went well," Walter continued. "But they're probably not going to be the ones that end up buying this place. A great couple, but I think the house was a little bigger than they had imagined from the pictures on the website."

"Wow, your house has only been for sale for a week and

you've already had a couple showings. That's pretty good isn't it?" Tom says, interested by the results of selling privately.

"Yes, I think it is," Walter says confidently. "I've also had six to eight calls and three or four emails from interested buyers that could turn into actual showing appointments. There is a definite interest in the house. And people are finding out it's for sale."

"Well, now that we are going to have to sell our house and upgrade, we need to decide how we are going to list. I'm really playing with the idea of selling privately like you, but I think Julie would still like to go with her cousin Sam, the real estate agent." Tom shares his situation with Walter.

"I still have a few questions on the whole private sale thing, but I think if I can get comfortable enough with it, and come up with a strong game plan, Julie will buy into it. The family relation to the agent makes it tough, but the money we'd save by not using an agent could sway her in the private sale direction.

"Do you know how all these people found your house? Did they see your sign and call?" Tom asks.

"Why don't you come in for a few minutes and I'll get you something to drink? We can tell Carole about your news too." Walter suggests.

"That'd be great," Tom says, excited to learn more about Walter's current experience.

As Tom follows Walter into the house, Carole is just leaving. Walter shares the news of the twins with her. She is extremely happy for them. She gives Tom a hug and mentions that she will call Julie later to congratulate her on their news. She says goodbye to the men and continues on out the door.

"What can I get you to drink, Tom?" Walter asks.

"I would love a Diet Coke," Tom replies, knowing that Walter is an avid Diet Coke drinker and always has some in his house.

"Good choice," Walter replies with a grin. "Coming right up."

They make their way to the kitchen. There are a few bill statements, a seller's disclosure document and some feature sheets lying on the table. Walter organizes them into their own piles and sets them aside to make room for their drinks.

"So you were asking about how these people found our house," Walter recapitulates as he sits down. "Well, the people that were in today said they found the house when they were searching on the PropertyGuys.com website.

"They said they like to visit that website once or twice a week and are always interested in what's available in their price range. When they saw the pictures of our house, they called up and wanted to see it. They really liked the virtual tour pictures. Once they arrived here, they said the tours were a great representation of the house. It gave them a great idea of what the rooms looked like before they got here."

"That's neat," Tom replies. "What about some of the other calls you got? How'd they know your house was for sale?"

"I know a few of them automatically received an email from PropertyGuys.com when my listing was added. I can't remember if we've talked about this before or not?" Walter says thinking back to their original conversation a week or so ago.

"I'm not sure I remember," Tom replies, "Maybe you can refresh my memory."

"Well, buyers that visit PropertyGuys.com can sign up to get an email when a house matching their criteria is added to their website. Buyers can select city, property type, price range, things like that, and when the company adds these types of properties to their website, the buyer will get an email of the seller's listing. The tool really helps match buyers and sellers," Walter explains.

"Yeah, that sounds like a really useful feature for both the buyer and the seller," Tom says.

"As far as the other callers go, I can't remember if I ended up asking them how they first found us. I know at least one of them saw the sign when they drove by the other day," Walter states. "You know, the professional lawn sign that PropertyGuys.com provides really sends a message of credibility and seriousness to buyers. I think buyers like dealing with people that are serious about selling their house, so that they aren't wasting their time with a seller that still isn't quite sure what they are doing."

Walter tries to remember back to the various phone conversations he's had with other potential buyers. "To be honest, I'm not sure how the others came across us. They may have just been visiting PropertyGuys.com and found our listing or talked to someone else they knew that had found it. I usually try and ask though, since I like to know what part of the program seems to be working the best.

"Actually, one of the calls this morning was from someone that had seen our classified ad in this morning's paper," Walter shares as the most recent phone conversation popped into his head. "When I listed with PropertyGuys.com, I chose the print advertising option. It costs a little more, but there are still a lot of people that like to check the newspaper classified ads for homes. I thought if I could combine classified ads with the power of the internet, that I would get maximum exposure for my house. You can never have your home listed in too many places."

"True enough," Tom replies. "I guess it's all about letting as many people know as possible."

Tom follows up his original question about how potential buyers are finding out about Walter's house. "When these people call you, how do you know if they are really interested in buying? Couldn't they just be wasting your time?"

"I suppose they could be," Walter replies. "But I've found that having all the pertinent information listed on the website really does a good job eliminating all the 'lookie loos' and 'tire-kickers' that are just curious about the house. Whatever information they are curious about — rooms, size, price — they can now find it on the internet. And that saves time on useless calls for the seller."

"That's why there is a big difference between selling privately with a well respected brand like PropertyGuys.com and selling 'For Sale by Owner' with an orange and black yard sign. It's all about getting information to the buyer. With PropertyGuys.com, all my information is available so a phone call is usually about setting up a showing. With the old 'For Sale by Owner' yard sign, the phone call is usually about getting preliminary information."

"So as you can tell, PropertyGuys.com essentially helps filter out unqualified buyers. I've talked to other home sellers that have tried to sell with the black and orange sign, only to have switched later to a private sale company. It's interesting because one of the things they told me was that when they switched, they actually received less calls on their home. But the calls that they did receive were from people that were much more interested in actually buying the house. These people seemed to be much further along in their decision-making process."

"Let me just also mention that there can be a difference between an interested buyer and a qualified buyer. Many times, a stumbling block to the completion of a sale is the pre-approval of a buyer for a specific mortgage amount. PropertyGuys.com partners with mortgage brokers across the country so that buyers and sellers can get access to mortgage financing. And if you give a showing to someone that has not yet got financing, you can always point them in the mortgage partner's direction."

Tom is finding this fascinating. He's even more intrigued now that he can see how it all might apply to his situation.

"So once you have a qualified buyer, they've seen the house and they're interested, how do you go about talking price and getting a deal?" Tom's curious as to how the transition takes place from viewing to negotiating. "Does the private sale company negotiate for you?"

"No, I get to negotiate myself," Walter replies. "I like doing this because I'll usually know whether a buyer is serious or not by the types of questions they ask. If they start asking things like 'how much are you asking for the house?' or 'what's included in the asking price?' or 'when do you think we could move in?', these are the types of questions that usually indicate they are wanting to talk about a deal."

"What if the buyer comes back with a lower price? Or they want something fixed first?" Tom asks.

"Well, that's really all part of the negotiation process," Walter says with a grin. "If they accepted your original terms, then there wouldn't be any negotiations."

"Once you are to this point, there's essentially three key pieces of information you need to get to the buyer: price, what's included at that price — appliances, fixtures, closing conditions, things like that — and a closing date.

"Negotiating is really nothing more than the buyer and seller exchanging offers and variations on these three key pieces of information until they either reach an agreement, or they decide that they can't reach an agreement. Negotiating can be done verbally — in person or on the phone — or written on a purchase and sale agreement. Once a written agreement is reached, the buyer typically puts down a deposit towards the selling price. This can be coordinated through your lawyer.

"While I get to stay in control of the negotiations by doing it myself, PropertyGuys.com does provide legal templates and access to a legal professional. Even when you use a real estate agent to help sell your house, you'll need a lawyer to help close the deal.

"Real estate lawyers become extremely important to coordinating offers, performing deed searches, calculating adjustments, conducting closing services, and other things like these. Actually, real estate services may vary from city to city, which makes it even more important to have a trusted legal professional working for you."

Just then the phone rings. Walter excuses himself and answers it. Tom looks at his watch and realizes he's been at Walter's place longer than he had intended. He stands up with the intention of heading to the door once Walter gets off the phone.

Tom can hear Walter's side of the conversation. The caller is someone interested in viewing his home. Walter looks over at Tom and gives him a wink and a grin. Tom can tell that Walter and the caller are trying to figure out the best time to show the house. They confirm a time for early next week and Walter hangs up the phone.

"My third confirmed showing," Walter says, grinning ear to ear. "I've got to admit, I didn't get this much action, this fast, the last time I listed privately. I guess it just goes to show that buyers are also looking at private sale homes as a place to buy their next house; it's really catching on.

"I also like the fact that I can set the best time for a showing. A lot of times, setting the showing times is not even about the exact time of their arrival, but rather about being able to tidy the house before they get here. This couple wanted to come over Tuesday night, but I know that I have to work late that night and Carole would be left here to get the house ready on her own. So we settled on Wednesday night instead.

"Listen, since you are still trying to figure out if you want to sell privately, why don't you come by for the showing on Wednesday? It's at seven o'clock. It might help you figure a few things out," Walter offers.

"I think I will." Tom replies, "We told Julie's cousin Sam that we would get back to him by next weekend, so this will definitely give me some insight and should help me make a more informed decision."

"I'll see you then, Tom," Walter says as Tom lets himself out the front door.

"See you later," Tom replies.

6
The Showing

Tom's been looking forward to this day ever since Walter invited him over for the showing. Through talking with Walter, he's become fairly comfortable with most of the process of selling a home privately, but he's extremely curious to see how a showing takes place.

It's about fifteen minutes before the prospects are to arrive at his neighbour's house. Tom heads over to Walter's place so he's not in the way once the potential buyers show up. Tom rings the doorbell and waits.

"Hi there, Tom," Walter says. "Glad you could make it over."

"Well thanks for letting me come by," Tom replies. "I've been looking forward to this. If I can get comfortable with the showing and negotiating, then I'm pretty sure I can handle this private sale thing."

"I'm sure you'll find there's nothing to it," Walter says calmly. "Why don't we sit in the kitchen; we'll be out of the way when the buyers go through the house."

"Sounds good," Tom replies.

Walter and Tom make their way to the kitchen table. Walter has a fresh pot of coffee on and the hazelnut blend fills the room.

"Cup of coffee, Tom?" Walter asks.

"That would be great," Tom replies.

Tom sees some documents Walter has lying around on

the table. He remembers them from the last time he was over, just after Walter's previous showing.

"I notice you have some papers here on the table," Tom says to Walter as he eyes the documents. "I remember seeing them when I was over after your last showing."

"Yeah, I like to have a few things ready for when the visitors show up. When they first come in, I like to get them to sign my guest registry. It is just an informal list of the people that have been through our house with their address and phone number, in case we need to get in touch with them.

"The last house we sold, we had a couple forget a set of keys in one of the rooms. The guest registry helped me get in touch with them. Come to think of it, they must have been the wife's keys because he was able to drive away from there."

"Anyway, once they sign the guest registry, I usually give them a copy of our feature sheet. It's essentially a print out of our PropertyGuys.com website listing. This way, a lot of the common questions will be answered as they go through the house."

"These other ones, such as our electric bills, disclosure document and purchase and sales agreement, I like to keep here until after the showing. Only if they are really interested will they usually ask to see any of this other information."

"They should be here anytime," Tom says just as the door bell rings. "Am I good or what?" he chuckles.

Walter heads over to the entry way. He opens the door and welcomes the couple into his home.

"Good evening folks," Walter says as he directs them into his house with an outstretched arm. "I'm Walter Williams. My wife Carole is out tonight, but she welcomes you into our home as well."

Walter takes each of their coats and hangs them in the closet.

"Well, thank you," the gentleman replies. "I'm George Taylor and this is my wife Susan."

"Hi George, hi Susan," Walter repeats each person's name as he shakes their hands. "Come on in."

"Let's head over to the kitchen. I've got a guest book I wouldn't mind having you sign and I'll give you a printed copy of the feature sheet for the house. Then, I'll leave you two to walk through the house so that you can openly discuss what you're seeing without having to worry about hurting my feelings."

"Oh, this is my neighbour Tom." Walter points toward Tom as the three of them enter the kitchen area. "He's thinking about selling privately and wanted to see how things happen during a showing. We've been good friends ever since he and his wife moved in next door a number of years ago."

"Tom, this is George and Susan Taylor."

Tom stands up to shake their hands, "Nice to meet you both."

"If you don't mind signing the guest book," Walter continues as he holds a pen out with one hand and directs them with the other. He hands the pen off to Susan who signs for both of them. "Here's a feature sheet." Walter gives the feature sheet to George as he waits for Susan to finish filling out their phone number.

Susan finishes signing the guest book and turns to face Walter and her husband.

"Let me just give you some general directions and then I'll let you go through the house on your own. As you can see, we're standing in the kitchen and eating area. To the left, we have a sitting area and, to the right and down this little hallway, we have a TV room. Going left or right will bring you to the front door where you came in. The garage is through that door." Walter points to a door off from the eating area they are in.

"As you probably noticed when you first walked in,

there is a flight of winding stairs which leads to three bedrooms and two full baths. One of those bedrooms is the master bedroom with a full bath and a walk-in closet. The other two bedrooms share the full bath in the hallway."

"Now, if you go right from here, toward the TV room, there is another set of winding stairs heading down to the lower level. Downstairs, you'll find a bedroom to your immediate right, a hallway to your left. Off the hallway are a storage closet and a laundry room. The hallway leads to a large living room with patio doors that take you to the backyard."

"Oh, by the way, when you are upstairs in the walk-in closet, be sure to check out the wooden cover on the right hand wall – it's a laundry chute which drops clothes down to the laundry room. If you look down the chute though, watch your head on the shelf above; I've knocked my head on it a few times." Walter says with a chuckle, as he rubs his head at the spot he generally hits.

"Enough of listening to me, I'll let you get right to the tour. If you have any general questions, I'll be right here at the table. If you want to ask me a question about something you see, feel free to give a holler and I'll come and meet you." Walter says in his kind voice. Walter's personality makes everyone feel at home around him.

"Thanks Walter," George says as he and Susan turn toward the cupboards in the kitchen. They take a few steps, stop and begin their tour. Walter and Tom stay quiet while they survey the kitchen and cupboard areas."

"Quick question before we move to the next room," George says, as he turns back toward Walter, "I see on the feature sheet that the appliances are negotiable. I assume that the list price you have here does not include the appliances?"

"That's correct," Walter replies, "The appliances are only a few years old and are still in great working condition. We're unsure if the buyer would want them or not, so we chose to leave them out of the price. But if you want them, we can always negotiate them in."

"Sounds good," George turns back with his wife. Susan takes a pen out of her purse and makes some notes on the feature sheet. They take a few more seconds to look around before they move to the next room down the hall.

"So you don't show the visitors around when they come to see your home?" Tom asks, somewhat surprised.

"No. Typically I'll give them direction on where to go, but I often find that people want to look around and have the freedom to talk about the things they see," Walter replies. "Sometimes I offer to take them around, especially if someone comes by themselves, but usually I'll just leave them alone to see things for themselves."

"Now, if they are looking for certain things such as electrical panels or water valve shutoffs, then I'll definitely show them. But you do have to give them their space," he continues.

"Do you ever worry about anybody stealing anything?" Tom asks.

"You always want to have your valuables locked away somewhere for everyone's protection." Walter replies, "You can also do some things to protect yourself as well. I ask for people's names and phone numbers, but you could also sneak a peak out at their license plate number and write that down somewhere. Generally, people aren't going to be that brave when there are others in the house. You definitely want to have all of your valuables stored away where visitors aren't seeing them."

"Really, it's no different than when a real estate agent brings someone through; especially if it's a buying agent and their clients. Sellers are strongly encouraged to leave during showings. When a buying agent brings their clients through, you might not know any of the people going through your house. Either the agent or their clients may be untrustworthy; who's to know these days. You would have to protect your valuables just as much in these types of situations. You would want to have them put away somewhere safe."

"I suppose that would really be the case when the agent holds an open house," Tom says as he relates this experience to some of the agent showings and open houses he's been to. "There would be so many different people through that it would be tough for an agent to keep an eye on them all. I guess this really isn't much different when you stop and think about it."

"Did you say before that you won't hold any open houses? That you will only show based on appointments?" Tom inquired.

"That's right. In my opinion, open houses are really guess work, and from what I've seen, a prospecting tool that real estate agents have invented to try and sign up more clients for themselves," Walter says without any malice. "With my PropertyGuys.com web listing, I consider myself to be holding an open house on the internet 24/7.

"With all the property information, still photos, and virtual tours I have on the internet, people seeing my property listing will have a pretty good idea as to whether or not they are interested. If they are interested, then I know that they will get in touch with me by email or phone. If they are not interested, then they will move on to the next home. I'm not sure an open house will motivate anyone beyond these two options.

"Now, I'm not saying they would never work, I've just never been very big on them," Walter clarifies his position. He's not against them, he's just decided that he's not going to bother with them because of his past experience.

"I guess it stems back to the time I had listed with an agent. I think I was telling you that the first few weeks were fine. Well, I don't think I told you that, toward the end, our agent wasn't even the one doing our open house. Our agent would send the new person from the office to do his open houses for him. We dropped in one time and this new agent was just sitting there taking names of new people and handing out his business cards. I heard him say a few times that he wasn't sure of an answer because he was showing the home for another agent. I heard 'I'll get back to you on that' a couple times that afternoon. Not great representation if you ask me."

Just then, George had come to the top of the downstairs' staircase. "Walter, do you have a second? We have a question about something in the backyard. We caught a glimpse of it through the patio doors down here."

"Sure thing," Walter replied. "I'll be right there."

Walter followed George down the stairs, down the hallway and through the living room. "Walter, we noticed a few dirt holes in the back by the house. Are there any animals that live in the neighbourhood that dig up your back yard? Raccoons? Skunks?"

"Oh, those holes were made by my son's terrier," Walter sighs, shaking his head back and forth while cracking a smile, "The only time we have an animal problem is when that dog is around."

His son's terrier is quite the energetic little fellow and loves to dig in the dirt when he visits. "No, there really aren't many animals in the neighbourhood. I've never seen a raccoon or a skunk in all the six years I've lived here."

"I know the 'hole' question may have seemed like a bizarre one, but we lived in a house that had a terrible raccoon problem. They'd always get in our garbage and be such a nuisance. We would hate to get back into a situation like that," George replied.

"Oh, while I have you down here Walter," George continued, "We noticed the air exchanger in the laundry room. When did you last have that looked at? I think they are suppose to be serviced every year or so and I'm just curious when we would need to have that looked at again."

"We had someone in here about six months ago for a

routine cleaning. We try to get someone in here every twelve to eighteen months or so. I think I still have the receipts for the service if you want to look at them," Walter replied. "I'm pretty sure I have them filed with the other general maintenance receipts."

"Great, don't worry about them right now," George replies. "But we may ask for them if we decide to go further."

"No problem," Walter said. "Anything else at the moment, or would you like me to leave you to continue?"

"I think we are almost finished. We are going to head out to the garage and then take a look at the back deck."

George and Susan follow Walter up the stairs to the main floor to get their coats.

"Why don't you take a look at the back deck first?" Walter suggests. "When you're finished out back, you can then go to the garage, and we can meet at the side door that comes through to the eating area. Actually, we'll probably see you through the patio doors."

"Sounds like a plan," says George.

Walter meets Tom back at the table. "How did that go?" Tom asks Walter, curious as to the types of questions that got asked.

"It went fine. They had questions about a hole in the ground out back and the air exchanger." Walter replied

"A hole in the ground?" Tom is clearly puzzled.

Walter is laughing as he replies: "Yeah, they wanted to know if we had an animal problem because there was a big hole dug in the back. I told them our only animal problem is my son's terrier." Walter continues laughing.

"That crazy dog; he's all over the place." Tom says as he chuckles at Walter's comments. Tom has caught the terrier in his yard the odd time when Walter's son had been at his place visiting.

"They also asked about the last time the air exchanger was serviced," Walter continues, "Both things I was very comfortable answering."

"They always say that no one knows a home better than the home owner, and I would agree one hundred percent," Walter states, backing up his previous comments. "That's why I'm so comfortable showing my home. I know an agent wouldn't have been able to answer either of those questions the Taylors asked. The agent would have ended up getting the answers from me. By selling without an agent, I'm just skipping that middle step.

"See, there really are no difficult questions. And if by some chance they do ask something that should stump you, you can always say you'll look into it and get back to them."

"I guess you're right," Tom says with relief. "I guess I'm really worrying over nothing."

Tom and Walter finish their coffee. From his seat at the table, Walter watches the Taylors on the deck through the patio windows. Tom is more convinced now than ever that he wants to sell privately. He starts to think about how he is going to convince Julie that this is the best for the family.

The Taylors have moved to the garage. Tom is still deep in thought. Walter is shuffling the papers on the table in preparation of the Taylors showing more interest. Both are interrupted by the knock at the side door into the garage.

"There they are," Walter says as he gets up to answer the door. "The moment of truth," he says quietly as he passes by Tom.

Walter opens the door and George and Susan walk into the kitchen.

"So how did it go?" Walter asks with a smile. "Did you get a chance to see everything you were looking for?"

"Your house is lovely," Susan replies, "Your virtual tours on the PropertyGuys.com website really did a great job at presenting your home. I felt like this was our second time going through the house."

Walter realized that he hadn't yet asked about how they found out his house was for sale.

"Oh, did you find my house online?" he asks.

"Actually, we saw your ad in the classified section of the newspaper the same day we called — Saturday I think. The ad made reference to the website along with an ID number. Since your address was included in the ad, we knew we liked this part of town, so we decided to go online and get more information. The website listing gave us all the information we were looking for and the pictures and virtual tour were amazing," Susan continued. "So I got George to give you a call so we could come see it."

"We've been looking at moving for some time," George added. "But we just hadn't found the right place. We really weren't in a hurry, so we didn't need to rush. We really like what we see here. Susan and I will probably need a little time to talk, but I'm sure we'll be in touch to see what we can work out.

"Do you have a copy of your energy bills, your tax bill and the air exchanger service receipt? We'd like to verify quickly what some of the expenses are here. We might write a few numbers down so we can look at them later."

"No problem. Here are copies of the heating bills," Walter says as he gathers the bills from the table and hands them to George. Susan pulls a pen and notepad out of her purse and takes the receipts from George. She starts writing down the monthly power bill totals for the previous twelve months.

"I'll need to run down to the filing cabinet to get copies of the other two things for you. Oh, while I'm down there, George, here's a copy of our seller's disclosure document. It outlines the current condition of the property. You can take a look at it while I'm getting those other receipts for you." Walter slides the seller's disclosure document across the table to George. George picks it up and scans through the details.

George is impressed by the seller's disclosure document, which allows him to quickly review the state of the home. The Taylors have visited a number of homes for sale since they started looking, and not every one of them had a detailed seller's disclosure document; not even all of the homes represented by real estate agents. Most agents will only present this document at the time of the offer, so a buyer won't be able to take this information into account until after they make an initial offer.

"I'll be right back," Walter runs downstairs to retrieve the bills the Taylors are asking about. He's fairly certain he knows right where those two file folders are. It takes him only a couple minutes to find the tax bills and service receipts.

"Here you go," Walter states as he returns to the eating area and hands the documents over. Susan flips her piece of paper over and writes down the annual tax number and the last service date, contractor and cost for the air exchanger service.

"Thanks, Walter," George says as Susan finishes writing down the last details. "If we do decide to place an offer, we're probably going to want to have a home inspector through the house just to make sure we haven't overlooked anything important."

"I don't see that as a problem," Walter replies, "I always like to make sure there are no hidden surprises as well. Should you make an offer, we can just make the inspection a condition of the sale."

"Well, we won't put the cart before the horse," George replies with a light grin, "Susan and I will do some talking and then we'll be in touch."

"Sounds good," Walter replies. And he waves them off as they leave through the garage. Walter shuts the door and returns to Tom.

"That wasn't so bad now was it," says Walter.

"No, not at all," Tom replies "Do you think you'll have

a deal here?"

"It's off to a good start, but it's still pretty early. We'll probably go back and forth a couple of times, and a deal will depend on where we end up. And the back and forth is not always about money. Sometimes it's about closing times, inspection clauses, home improvements, those types of things. We'll see where we end up," Walter replies.

Just then Carole returns home from her outing. The three of them get talking about the showing and then about the Allens and their upcoming twins. Carole is so excited for them. She could hear the excitement in Julie's voice when she spoke to her on the phone the other day. They spend about twenty minutes talking until Tom notices the time and feels he should be getting home.

"Well, thanks for letting me sit in on this," Tom says.

"No problem," Walter replies. "Let me know if there is anything else I can help you with."

Tom heads toward the door just as the phone starts ringing. Tom pauses for a moment and watches Walter pick up the phone.

"Hello?" Walter answers. It's the Taylors. They had discussed the house as they were driving home and wanted to put an offer in immediately.

Walter covers the receiver and mouths 'It's the Taylors' to Tom. He waves to Walter as he turns and continues out the door. Walter waves back. Tom smiles to himself as if he's just confirmed how he wants to approach the sale of his home.

7
The Dilemma

Tom leaves his neighbour's home with a lot on his mind. He and Julie have a huge decision to make about how to approach the sale of their home. On the one hand, he is excited about the things he's learned about selling privately. On the other, he knows his wife is loyal to Sam and would like to use him as their selling agent. They need to get an answer back to Sam over the next couple of days. Whatever they decide, it will have a large effect on their finances.

Tom returns home excited about how easy the showing went. He's learned a lot from spending time with Walter over the last week and a half. His preference is to sell privately. He'll now have to convince Julie of the same.

Tom arrives home in time to tuck Billy into bed. Julie was just finishing reading to him as Tom walked in to say good night. They kiss Billy on the forehead, shut out the light and proceed down the hall to the living room.

"How did the showing go tonight?" Julie started.

"The showing went great." Tom replied with enthusiasm, hoping he can win part of her over by showing a real zest for private sale. "I really couldn't believe how simple it was. Walter gave the visitors a feature sheet and some general directions on the layout of the house, and then let them go off on their own. During the showing, the visitors had a couple of questions, but nothing that would be considered difficult."

"I got to talk to Walter some more during the showing. He made a couple of good points when it came to real estate agents and showings.

"First, a lot of times it's not even the selling agent that is showing the home. It's either a substitute for the selling agent or it's the buying agent of the people that are looking to buy. In both of these cases, neither of these agents would be familiar with the house at all. And even if the selling agent is the one showing the home, most of the time, he's bringing questions to the seller to answer.

"And this leads directly to the second point; nobody knows a house better than the home owner. In a private sale, buyers can ask questions directly to the home owner. There's no need for the messenger. And I saw it work fine tonight in Walter's case.

"If you think back to when we bought this place, it wasn't the selling agent that brought us through, it was our agent. In fact, I don't think we ever saw the selling agent. And when we went through the house, our agent really didn't do much more than open the door and point out what room was what. There really wasn't much selling on his part other than saying it was a nice house in a nice neighbourhood."

"Yes, but we really didn't ask him many questions," Julie replies, thinking back to when they went through the house for the first time.

"That's fair enough," Tom admits. "But I guess I'm pointing out that the agent didn't provide much value at the showing. Really, anyone could have pointed out that the room with the toilet was the bathroom." Tom laughs at his own joke.

"I suppose you're right," Julie says with a little bit of a smile. "But Sam can use his industry connections to find us potential buyers. He always says he has access to buyers."

"Listen honey, I like Sam," Tom says, laying a friendly

foundation for what he is about to say. "But he's only been a real estate agent for a couple months. During that time, he might have landed a couple of listings, but I don't think he has sold anything yet has he? That's not saying much about his connections or his access to buyers."

"I know," Julie reluctantly agrees, "but he's just starting in the business.

"Really, I'm most concerned that people won't know that our house is for sale. You know, over the last couple of days, I talked to one of the girls at work about selling privately. She said that she and her husband had bought one of those orange and black signs for the front yard and tried to sell on their own. They ended up going with a real estate agent after a couple of weeks. This is pretty much what Sam says also. Selling on your own isn't all that successful. I don't want us to waste our time on this.

"Plus, Sam can get us on the multiple listing service."

"I would agree that if we just bought a sign for our front yard that we are probably not going to be seen by enough people to make it work. Doing it alone without any marketing help we would probably be unsuccessful as well. That's really the old way of selling privately, with the lonely old 'For Sale by Owner' sign on the front yard," Tom admits.

"But there is really a new way of selling privately. And that is what Walter is benefiting from. He's using PropertyGuys.com to help him market his home. With the right marketing tools and support, I'm confident we can gain enough exposure to get our house noticed by buyers.

"Private sale companies specialize in marketing private sale homes. A company like PropertyGuys.com will put a professional sign on the front lawn to attract people that drive by, offer classified advertising to get in front of the people that still look in the newspaper for homes for sale, and provide a polished website that buyers will find and visit."

"Remember the other night when Sam was over and we talked about selling privately?" Tom asks. "Did you know that the company Walter is listed with is a national private sale company?

"PropertyGuys.com has locally owned offices all across the country. They are getting millions of hits every month. Buyers are finding houses on their website and people are buying homes they have listed. The company is spending a lot of time and energy promoting their clients' homes to buyers on the internet.

"With millions of website hits a month, it's clear that the multiple listing service is not the only real estate site that people are checking when looking for houses. PropertyGuys.com is not doing so bad itself. Have you been to their website?" Tom asks.

"Actually, I haven't," Julie replies.

"Well, let's go check it out. We'll look up Walter's listing," Tom says. "Can you see Walter's ID number on the sign from the front window?"

Julie gets up and looks out the window but because of that big evergreen tree in Walter's front lawn, she can barely see the sign at all. "That stupid tree is in the way," she mutters as she peers out the window, "I can't see the ID number."

"That's okay," says Tom. "We can find it through their listing search."

Tom and Julie head downstairs to their computer. Tom pulls up a second chair so Julie can get a good look at the monitor. He rolls up the office chair and types in www.propertyguys.com.

Tom lands on the PropertyGuys.com website and finds the property search area. He searches by city to find all the homes in their area. His search returns multiple pages of homes for sale. They are both impressed with the number of homes PropertyGuys.com has listed. They didn't realize just how popular selling privately really is.

As they scroll through all the homes, Julie spots Walter's listing by the picture of the front of his house in the search results section. "There it is," Julie exclaims as she points to the picture of Walter's home on the screen. Tom clicks on the image to get more details.

"There is quite a bit of detail to the listing," Julie comments. "There are plenty of photos and I bet the virtual tour is pretty popular for those looking to buy a home."

"You're probably right," Tom agrees. "I can see why Walter says the prospects that end up giving him a call tend to be serious about wanting to see the house. With all the details and pictures, you can really get a good feel for what a house has to offer."

"I can see how that would be," Julie admits. "Can Walter tell how many people have looked at his listing online?"

"Yes, that's one of the features of listing with PropertyGuys.com. He can tell how many people have viewed his home on the website," Tom replies.

Tom and Julie take a look at a couple virtual tours while they're on the information page.

"Wow, the virtual tours are a nice touch," Julie says as she watches one of Walter's tours pan around his living room, "It sure helps to get some perspectives on the rooms."

"Is that something we would have to do?" she asks Tom.

"No, a PropertyGuys.com representative takes the virtual tour pictures and puts them up on the website for us," Tom replies. "They also take the still photos and put the sign up as well."

Tom starts clicking around on the company's website. He finds the registration area where he can access all the site tools.

"Here's the area where buyers can join up to access website tools such as listing notifications and the favorites area," Tom says as he eyes the login and registration page. "I think I'm going to sign up; it'll only take a minute."

Tom enters his information and logs into the site. "See, after you sign in, you can register for the new listing emails. This feature allows you to put in the details of the type of property you are looking for and if a listing gets added to the website that matches what you've entered then you get an email with the listing's ID number. Walter has already received emails from people that found his home this way."

"And there's a place you can save your favorite listings," Tom states.

"You know, Tom, we should take a look at some of the listings they have on this website and sign up to these buyers tools," Julie offers. "After all, we are in the market for a new house."

"That's a great idea," Tom exclaims.

Tom enters the information about the type of house they are looking to buy. As he fills out the form, a few other thoughts come into his mind. He starts sharing them with Julie.

"One of the reasons I really like PropertyGuys.com so much is because they actually have people in the area that can help. I was doing a little bit of research the other night while you were in bed and I noticed that a lot of these private sale or 'For Sale by Owner' companies are just virtual companies, just internet listings with very little support beyond a listing. This company is different.

"Plus, when I looked for them on the internet through search engines, they were easy to find," Tom finished.

"Well, how much does it cost?" Julie asks, thinking it's still going to be pricey if they have representatives in the area and they come and set you up.

"That's the great part. It's only a few hundred dollars. We would pay this one-time, flat-fee up front, but then once we sold the house, we would get to keep all the money from the sale."

"If we went with Sam, our commission would be over ten thousand dollars – plus tax! That's ten thousand dollars we can keep in our pockets, instead of Sam's pocket, the buying agent's pocket and their two brokers' pockets. I'd much rather keep it in ours.

"Ten thousand dollars is a lot of money. People play the lottery to win that much. It would take the average income earner three or four months to clear that amount. It's really no small sum.

"And do you know what we could do with that kind of money? That's a brand new kitchen, or all new appliances. It's a new big screen television with a high end sound system. We could take the family on a vacation. Trade in our car and upgrade to a mini-van or sports utility vehicle. We could invest it into registered savings plans for our retirement years. There are a number of smart things we could do with the money."

"The savings are impressive," Julie admits, "But I will feel really bad for Sam if we decide not to use him. I've been handing out his cards to just about everyone I know that was selling real estate."

"But those people were looking for an agent," Tom says. "And you handed them Sam's card. A lot of people still don't realize they can sell privately. Look at us. Two weeks ago we wouldn't have been talking about private sale either."

"Let's at least give it a try. When you look at the cost of listing, it's only a fraction of the commission we would have to pay. If for whatever reason we can't pull it off, we can always list with Sam later. That's what we'll tell him, that we want to give private sale a try, but that if we decide we want to get our house on the multiple listing service, then we will give him a call and he can take our listing."

"Plus, we'll let him know that we will use him as our buying agent if we buy a home listed with an agent. This way, we won't have to completely turn him down. I think he'll like that," Tom says, happy he thinks he's found a compromise for their Sam situation.

"You do realize I'm pregnant and won't be able to help you much," Julie replied, looking down at her belly. "You'll have to take the lead on this."

"I realize that. Really, it's not that much more work than what we would have to do if we listed with Sam. The biggest things we'll have to do are clean and maybe stage the home; and we'd want to do these things even if Sam was involved. These are presentation steps that are important no matter how we choose to list our home.

"I've seen Walter in action, and I'm sure I can do it," Tom says confidently. "Plus, Walter's only a phone call away."

"So what's the next step?" Julie asks.

"Well, I can call PropertyGuys.com tomorrow and see where we go from there," Tom replies. "Let's see what happens."

Tom and Julie call it a night. It will be a big day tomorrow for Tom. He's going to take his first step toward selling his own home. He's excited and nervous all at the same time. But he can't wait to save all that money.

8
The Deal

Tom gets up the next morning ready to take on the world. He has managed to convince Julie that they should sell privately. His next step is to call and book an appointment with PropertyGuys.com. He'll give them a call when he gets a minute at the office.

That time comes around lunch hour. He looks up the local PropertyGuys.com representative's phone number on the company's website. He picks up the phone and makes the call.

"Good afternoon, PropertyGuys.com, Barb speaking."

Tom is greeted by an upbeat, cheerful, professional voice at the other end of the line. It's always such a nice way to begin a conversation.

"Good day," Tom replies, catching the enthusiasm Barb has conveyed. "My wife and I are looking for information on selling our house privately."

"Well, great, you've called the right place," Barb replies. "Are you familiar with how our system works?"

"Somewhat, I guess," Tom says, not wanting to give her the wrong answer. "Maybe you could give me a quick overview."

"With pleasure," Barb responds.

"My name is Barb Young, and I'm the local PropertyGuys.com representative here in town. We give people the confidence and control to sell their home on their own, and help them save thousands of dollars in real estate commission. We provide home sellers with all the tools and support necessary to sell successfully."

"We would start by booking an appointment for me to come and meet with you at your home. At that time, we would determine which package would be the best for your situation, go over the steps to selling privately, record your property details, take the necessary pictures for the still images and virtual tours, and then put the sign up in the front yard. I can guide you through the whole process of getting setup with us. What do you think?"

"I think it sounds good," Tom replies. "And using your system, there are no commissions charged when the house sells, right?"

"That's right," Barb says. "Our system is completely flat-fee driven – no commissions. You keep all your money once your house sells. I can go over all the details if you would like to get together and meet."

"So, when can we set up an appointment?" Tom inquires.

"Well, I have a couple clients I need to set up tonight. I know tomorrow is the start of the weekend, but if you would like, I could come over tomorrow evening."

"That could work. How long does it take to get our house on the internet?" Tom asks.

"We can usually get you setup on the website within 24 hours," Barb replies. "It sounds like you already know that you want to list. If that's the case, I can get your phone number now and have the lawn sign ready for when I come over to meet with you. This way, we could get your sign up immediately. It would then be just a matter of getting your property information uploaded to the website. I could do that as soon as I returned to my home office. If we did this, I could have you set up within a matter of a couple of hours."

"That would definitely work," Tom replies, impressed

by the turnaround time that Barb can offer. "That would also give me tonight to get the house in order for the still photos and the virtual tours. Let's do that."

Tom gives Barb his name, address and phone number so she can get the sign ready. They set an appointment for Friday night at 6:30. Tom is pleased with the call and eager to get the process started. He calls Julie at the office to give her the good news.

Friday night seems to arrive quicker than Tom had anticipated. Thursday night was filled with packing, tidying and cleaning the house. Their goal was simply to remove some of the obvious clutter with the first go round of the house. They wanted to make sure the rooms were ready for picture taking once Barb showed up.

It was a lot of work, but they realized it was a necessary step no matter how they decided to sell their house. Her real estate agent cousin, Sam, would have required the same effort to get the house ready.

Tom and Julie's doorbell rang just before the scheduled appointment time. Tom ran down to get the door.

"Good evening, I'm Barb," she says with a smile and an outstretched hand, "You must be Tom."

"I am," Tom replies as he reaches out to shake her hand. "Come on in."

Barb enters the home with her notepad and information kit tucked under her arm. As she walks into Tom's home, she places her materials on the second step so she can remove her jacket and shoes.

"You've got a lovely home," Barb comments. "This is such a nice neighbourhood."

Tom takes Barb's jacket and hangs it in the closet. He takes Barb into the kitchen to meet his wife.

"Barb, this is my wife Julie," Tom says, introducing the two ladies.

"Nice to meet you, Julie," Barb says grinning.

"You as well," Julie replies.

"And if you see a little guy running around, his name is Billy. I think he's in his room playing at the moment, but he'll probably be around here sooner or later," Tom interjects.

"We can sit at the table," he continues as he directs Barb to the dining room table. "Would you like some coffee?"

"If it's already brewed that would be great," Barb replies, "but don't go through any special trouble. I'm fine really."

"It's no trouble at all," Tom replies. He turns the pot on to percolate as he gathers the cream and sugar to put on the table. He joins Barb and his wife as they begin their discussions. Barb opens her information kit.

"I'd like to begin by saying 'thank you' for calling me," Barb starts. "It seems like there are more and more people that are interested in selling privately these days. I've received so many calls lately. Have you ever sold your own home before?"

"No, we haven't," Tom replies. "We really just learned that selling privately was a feasible option. Actually, we found out from our neighbour Walter. He's listed with you also. I've spent some time over there helping him get his house ready to sell. I even sat in on one of his showings the other night."

"Oh, so you heard about us through Walter." Barb says as she makes the connection, "Well that makes sense. You know, private sale has really grown in this city over the last year or so that I've had the business. And most of my new clients have been referrals from old clients that have sold their home through our system. We've had a lot of satisfied clients. Word of mouth is our best form of advertising.

"Speaking of satisfied, Walter hasn't had his listing up very long, but I noticed on the website that he is getting a lot of people looking at his house on the internet. Since you guys are fairly close, he probably wouldn't mind me sharing this with you: his property received over 220 views in the first week alone. He was real happy when I told him that."

"Wow, that is pretty exciting," Tom says. "He did say he was getting a lot of calls and emails on his house. I can see why now."

"It's really been the same way across the country as well," Barb continues. "Our website hit numbers continue to grow month by month and we keep adding new franchise locations to the system. It's so exciting being part of this whole real estate revolution. I just love helping people keep their hard-earned equity. Last year alone, I've saved my clients over $750,000 in commissions; and that's just in our local area. That's a lot of money in homeowners' pockets.

"Now, we're going to help you save money.

"Since this is your first time selling privately, let me briefly go over the steps you'll need to take to complete the process and what you can expect. Feel free to stop me at any time and ask any questions you want. Sound good?"

Both Tom and Julie nod their heads in agreement.

"The first thing we are going to do is take the information down about your house. I've got a listing form that we can go through and fill out. Once we have the details filled out, I'll start taking photos of your house. We usually take pictures of the front of the house, the main bedrooms, bathrooms, dining room, kitchen and living room. If there are any special photos that you'd like me to take, you can let me know once we go through the house."

"I'll also select a couple of rooms to do a virtual tour. The virtual tours are really nice as they present a panoramic view of the different rooms in your house."

"We've seen a couple examples on the website," Tom says. "They are really a nice touch. Do they take long to put together?"

"Not at all," Barb answers him. "You'll be surprised

how quickly we'll get through them. I simply take sequential photos of a room, and then 'stitch' those together when I get back to the office. It's really interesting technology.

"Once I have all the details of your house, and the photos have been taken, I'll get you to sign an advertisement agreement and privacy policy. The advertisement agreement simply details the price and payment method for the services. The privacy policy outlines that we will only be using your information to provide you with the services we've agreed on."

"Do you take credit cards?" Tom asks.

"We do," Barb replies. "We take Visa, MasterCard or a personal check; whatever is most convenient for you.

"After we get the advertising agreement and the privacy policy signed, we can then get your sign up on the front lawn. The sign will have your phone number on it, a toll-free number to our national automated voice message system, and a unique ID number that people will be able to use to find your details online or access your voice message."

"I'll set up both your website listing and your automated telephone message as soon as I get back to the office tonight. If you choose to go with our print option, which I highly recommend, I would also get your ads ready based on the details of your web listing and run them in the local classified section. I can give you the schedule of when your ad would run in the newspaper."

"Your property ID number also allows you to do some additional marketing for your home if you wish. Just include the company's website address and your unique ID in any advertising you might do and people will be able to find your home quickly on our website."

"This essentially gets your listing ready, which is the first step in the whole process. Any questions so far?" Barb asks.

"Once the listing gets up there, is there any way to

change the information?" Tom asks.

"Definitely," Barb continues. "You can give me a call and I can change it for you. There is some information in the listing that you can change for yourself, price for example. You can update some of these fields online with a username and password. I can help you get that set up."

"Will we be able to know how many people see our listing online?" Julie asks.

"Yes, we track the number of times your specific property details page has been viewed. Again, you will be able to get that number through me at any time or you can log into your property details and get that number yourself," Barb replies. "We try to be as transparent as possible with respect to the details of your listing. After all, today's buyers want to learn as much as they can about a property before having to speak with someone about it.

"Once your listing is up and people start realizing that your house is for sale, you're going get phone calls. This is really the second major step in the whole process. Taking calls and arranging showings.

"To be honest, the first bunch of calls that you are going to get will be from real estate agents that want to get your listing. While some of them are well intentioned, most of them will try to tell you that they can sell your house faster and get more money for you. Interestingly enough, the last study we read on home sales contradicts these real estate agent assertions. The report concludes that most private sellers will in fact sell their home slightly faster and will receive a little more money than they would if they listed and sold through an agent.[1] I can get you a copy of this study if you are interested in seeing it."

"I wouldn't mind seeing that report," Julie replies interested in the findings. These are some of the facts that Sam tells his prospects. She would like to read the study to see what it has to say on the matter.

"No problem," Barb responds. "How about I email you

a copy of the report summary along with the source? The study was performed by an independent company for the real estate industry. Actually, one of the co-founders of the company is a licensed real estate agent. The results are really interesting."

"You might get a call from an agent who says they have an interested buyer for your home. Sometimes this is just a ploy to try and get your listing, while other times it may be a valid lead. One of the things that we recommend if you are interested in pursuing a lead like this from a real estate agent, is to negotiate a buy side commission only with them based on this one time showing. The buy side commission would typically be much lower than the average two sided commission where there is both a buying agent and a selling agent in the transaction. Agree with the agent that you are more than willing to pay that commission for these specific buyers only. They may want you to sign a document, but make sure the agreement is specific to this instance and this buyer, and not a longer term deal."

"Anyway, we just like to let our clients know that real estate agents will call and try to get your listing. It will always be your decision on how you want to sell your home, but we wanted to at least let you know that it's not unusual for these calls to occur."

"You will also begin to get phone calls from interested buyers," Barb continues. "Now, because potential buyers that reach you through our system have probably already seen how much you are asking, have seen all the images and virtual tours, and have access to a detailed description of your property, they tend to be more serious than someone that is calling without all this prior knowledge. Our system in general has a tendency to weed out the merely curious, because they can generally get all the information they are looking for on the web.

"I should also mention at this point that it becomes important to check your email. Because a lot of potential buyers will find your listing on the internet, they will often make their first contact through email. You won't want to miss out on these requests.

"So, when interested buyers call or email, they usually either have a list of more detailed questions, or they want to set up a time to come by and see your house. Selling privately allows you to control the appointment time and the showing. You'll end up setting an appointment time that is convenient for both you and the interested party.

"Of course, you'll want to make sure the house is in great showing condition. Make sure all the clutter is put away and that the house is presentable. There are actually 'home staging' companies that will come in and help you get your house ready for showing; that's an option as well. A lot of people feel they can do this on their own, but I thought I would mention that there is help out there, in case you were interested."

"How much does a professional home staging cost?" Tom asks.

"Really, it would depend on the services you wanted," Barb replies, "They can do everything from help you rearrange a room all the way to removing your furniture and bringing in some more modern pieces to update the house. They really do provide a full range of services. I can recommend someone to you if you're interested.

"The third step begins when you get an interested buyer and they begin to talk about price. This tends to lead to an offer being made. Our company can help by providing a few legal documents that can be used as a guide through this process.

"The seller's disclosure document, and the legal templates are the two main documents we provide. The seller's disclosure document outlines the status and condition of a number of the home's features. The legal templates essentially outline what information needs to be exchanged for a deal to be struck.

"Typically, negotiations revolve around the price of the house, what's included in the price – like fixings, appliances, conditions, and other things like that – and the closing date.

"We highly recommend that you involve a real estate lawyer once you get to this point. I've stapled a copy of our legal partner's business card to the top corner of the legal templates. When you start using this document, you should give them a call. They can answer any legal questions you might have. They're really familiar with private sale.

"Home sellers sometimes get to this point and think of the legal fees as an extra cost to selling privately. Realistically, legal costs are an expense that you would incur regardless of whether you sell privately or with an agent. It's simply necessary to finalizing a real estate transaction.

"You'll also want to make sure that the interested buyers are pre-qualified for a mortgage and can pay for the house once you reach an agreement. Before getting a lawyer involved, you may want to make sure this is the case. If the buyers indicate they haven't spoken to their bank or mortgage broker, then you may want to direct them to our mortgage broker partner in this area. They can help the buyer get pre-approved for a mortgage. I'll leave you some contact information for our mortgage broker partner.

"One last thing before we move to writing your information down and taking photos of the house. Do you know how much you want to ask for your house?" Barb asks.

"We do actually," Tom replies. "We had met with Julie's cousin who is a real estate agent and he told us how he would price the house. It was pretty close to the number I had in mind. I knew what we paid for the house about three years ago, and then I essentially took a look around to see how other similar homes were being priced. I did my own market analysis."

"Good for you," Barb responds. "That's how a lot of

people come up with their price. Since pricing is so important to the successful sale of a home, we like to suggest a real estate appraiser to those that aren't sure how to set an accurate price. You sound like you have this all under control."

"I think so," Tom says. "We might be at the top of the range, but I think I'm comfortable with using this as the starting point. You did say we could change this if we wanted to right?"

"That's right," Barb replies. "Price can be updated at any time."

"Well, that is essentially the process of selling your home. Any questions?" Barb asks as she begins to wrap up the process.

"I don't think so," Tom replies. "Do you have any questions, Julie?"

"No, other than getting a copy of that report, I'm fine." Julie replies.

"No problem at all, I've made myself a note to email that report to you." Barb scribbles down a note on the listing form.

"Sounds good," Tom says. "Well, this definitely confirms a lot of the things I've heard from Walter. I'm glad you went through the entire procedure though. It was good to hear it from A to Z."

"That's great," Barb says reassuringly. "I'm really glad you are feeling comfortable with the whole process."

"There is one little bit of information I haven't told you yet," Barb says to the couple with a sheepish grin. "This appointment with you worked out great for me since I can kill two birds with one stone. I got a call from Walter this afternoon. He wanted me to stop by and put the 'SOLD' sticker on his sign. I told him that it would be no problem since I'd be in the neighbourhood."

"Walter sold his house?" Tom said with surprise.

"Yes, he said that someone was by on Wednesday night

and they spent the next day or so negotiating the details of the agreement. They both signed off on the agreement today," Barb shared.

"Really? I was with Walter on Wednesday when he showed the house. I've met the people that will be moving in," Tom says with excitement. "I'll have to give him a call to congratulate him."

"So, are we ready to get started?" Barb asks Tom and Julie.

"Definitely, let's do it." Tom states enthusiastically.

9
The Result

True to her word, Barb had the Allen's home on the website and recorded on the automated telephone system within hours of her leaving their house. It was no time at all before they started receiving phone calls and emails from interested buyers. Julie even found herself getting caught up in the excitement of selling privately. She realized she enjoyed helping Tom with the showings; she liked meeting the people.

Despite the real estate market not being as strong as it had been earlier in the year, they still managed to successfully sell their home in just over four weeks, for the full asking price. And that was just the beginning of their exciting news that year. A few months later, Tom and Julie had a beautiful set of twin girls. They found a nice size two-story house in a flourishing neighbourhood.

The Allens and the Williams have remained good friends over the years and they often laugh as they share their private sale success stories and what they did with all the money they saved. Walter and Carole used their savings to put a down payment on a motorhome. They had always talked about traveling around the country for months at a time. Tom and Julie were able to purchase that mini-van they needed. Between the money they saved on the sale of the house and the trade in value of their four-door sedan, they were able to cover the entire cost of the brand new vehicle.

Now, four years later, the Allens find themselves wanting to move to the outskirts of town. Living in the packed neighbourhoods of the city is just too crazy. There's really no room in their yard for the kids to safely run and play. Tom often thinks back to when he was a child. His parents always had a large size lot with trees and green grass. He can remember running outside, chasing his friends around. He wants that for his kids now. So they've started looking for the right house to buy.

Tom and Julie have listed their house for sale once again. This time though, there was very little discussion on how they would do it. They called PropertyGuys.com and had their listing up as soon as they had made their decision.

Julie's friend Anne lives the next street over. The two women met when Julie began walking around the neighbourhood to get back into shape after the twins were born. She would often cross paths with Anne, walking roughly the same route through the maze of streets. They struck up a conversation one day, and have been walking together ever since.

Anne is driving past the Allen house for the first time after the 'For Sale' sign was installed and has to stop by to see what's going on. Julie is outside watering the plants in the front yard. She turns around to see her friend drive up the driveway and get out of the car.

"Julie, I saw the sign and had to stop. Are you moving?" Anne says in a shocked voice.

"Yes, we've decided we want to move somewhere a little outside of town; somewhere with a bigger yard for the kids to play in. We like this neighbourhood, but it's grown so much since we first moved in. It's getting too busy."

"Wow, I can't believe it. Do you know where you're moving to yet?" Anne inquires.

"No, not yet. We just had the sign put up last night. We

wanted to put our house for sale so that when we found something we liked, we'd already be in the process of selling our home."

Anne turns to take a good look at the 'For Sale' sign. "So who is your real estate agent?" she asks Julie. "My brother-in-law is an agent if you need one. I think I have one of his business cards in the car."

Anne turns to start toward her car.

"No, that's okay Anne," Julie replies, catching her before she gets too far. "We're selling our home privately."

"Oh, I wouldn't do that," Anne says with a look of concern. "My brother-in-law says that everyone needs an agent when they sell."

Julie has a flash of déjà vu and she starts to laugh out loud.

"What's so funny?" Anne asks Julie, grinning from the contagiousness of Julie's laughter.

"I'm sorry, Anne," Julie says as she catches herself, "I just had a flash back. This is four years ago all over again, except you are me and I'm my husband."

Ann stares at Julie with a look of confusion.

"Come on in. I'll explain," Julie continues with a grin as she leads Anne to the front door. "I once thought that myself. But I've since realized how to become a wealthy home seller."

Guides and Worksheets

How Much Money Can YOU Save?

Sale Price	5%	6%	7%
$50,000	$2,500	$3,000	$3,500
$60,000	$3,000	$3,600	$4,200
$70,000	$3,500	$4,200	$4,900
$80,000	$4,000	$4,800	$5,600
$90,000	$4,500	$5,400	$6,300
$100,000	$5,000	$6,000	$7,000
$120,000	$6,000	$7,200	$8,400
$140,000	$7,000	$8,400	$9,800
$160,000	$8,000	$9,600	$11,200
$180,000	$9,000	$10,800	$12,600
$200,000	$10,000	$12,000	$14,000
$220,000	$11,000	$13,200	$15,400
$240,000	$12,000	$14,400	$16,800
$260,000	$13,000	$15,600	$18,200
$280,000	$14,000	$16,800	$19,600
$300,000	$15,000	$18,000	$21,000
$325,000	$16,250	$19,500	$22,750
$350,000	$17,500	$21,000	$24,500
$375,000	$18,750	$22,500	$26,250
$400,000	$20,000	$24,000	$28,000
$425,000	$21,250	$25,500	$29,750
$450,000	$22,500	$27,000	$31,500
$475,000	$23,750	$28,500	$33,250
$500,000	$25,000	$30,000	$35,000
$550,000	$27,500	$33,000	$38,500
$600,000	$30,000	$36,000	$42,000
$650,000	$32,500	$39,000	$45,500
$700,000	$35,000	$42,000	$49,000
$750,000	$37,500	$45,000	$52,500
$800,000	$40,000	$48,000	$56,000
$900,000	$45,000	$54,000	$63,000
$1,000,000	$50,000	$60,000	$70,000

Protecting Your Equity

Equity Percent Cost Calculation

Example: Don and Deena are looking to sell their house. Their house has a market value of $210,000 and they have $150,000 left on their mortgage. A real estate agent has offered to sell their home for a 5% commission. Let's calculate what percentage of Don and Deena's equity they have to give up for the sale.

House Value		$210,000	**House Value**		$210,000
Mortgage	-	$150,000	**Commission %**	x	0.05
Equity	=	$60,000	**Commission**	=	$10,500

Equity % = **Commission** / **Equity** = $10,500 / $60,000

Equity % = 18%

Don and Deena's 5% commission is really costing them 18% of the equity they've built up in their home. Include the applicable taxes on the commission, and the equity percentage cost increases even further.

Equity Percent Cost Worksheet

What percentage of your equity would you end up paying in real estate commission?

House Value			**House Value**		
Mortgage	-	________	**Commission %**	x	________
Equity	=		**Commission**	=	

Equity % = **Commission** / **Equity** ________

Equity % = ________

Real Estate Myths Debunked *

Myth	Reality
Real estate agents will get you more money than if you sell on your own	People who sell privately generally make 6% more than those that use an agent; they make 29% more if you include the cost of the commission
Real estate agents will sell your home faster than if you sell it on your own	On average, agents took 11.5 weeks to sell a home, while private sellers took 8.1 weeks. Therefore, selling privately was on average 3 weeks faster than using an agent
Real estate agents didn't have to reduce the selling price as often as those that sold privately	Private sellers don't reduce their price as often as those people that are listed with a real estate agent
Real estate agents find buyers	People who sell privately believe their ability to find buyers is equal to or better than that of a real estate agent

* Realty ViewPoint was founded by a licensed real estate agent and provides real estate professionals with valuable consumer insights. In 2003, they performed a study of home sellers to determine their needs and the level of satisfaction with various aspects of the selling process. This table summarizes some of the results of their Home Sellers Consumer Insights: 2002-2003 report.

Setting Your Selling Price

One of the most important activities in selling your own home is pricing your home properly. Most home buyers use price as a key factor in determining which homes they want to pursue. As such, it is important to choose a pricing strategy that will deliver your desired result; a successful sale.

The most common mistake made by home sellers is overpricing. Some side effects of overpricing include buyers finding better deals at the price point you've set, the right buyer missing your home because it is not in the right price range and your home languishing on the market for an extended period of time. The ultimate end result of overpricing is a reduction in buyer interest.

Overpricing is often a result of:

- Seller paying a premium when home was purchased (i.e. bought in a high market)
- Trying to recover full costs from recent renovations
- Trying to maximize the amount of money from the sale (i.e. building in too much negotiation room)

If you are unsure as to how to properly price your home, there are a number of approaches you can use to help set your price. One of the best methods of pricing your home is to see what other comparable properties are currently on the market and pricing your home accordingly. One of the most traditional methods of determining the value of a home is to engage the services of a home appraiser.

Popular price setting methods:

- Research similar properties for sale in your area
- Compare your home against others in similar price range
- Get a professional appraisal
- Use an Automated Valuation Model (AVM)

The importance of pricing a home properly cannot be overstated. Setting the right price will attract more buyers and generate more offers.

A fair market price will:

- Increase market interest
- Expose the property to more buyers
- Prevent your home from languishing on the market
- Make your marketing campaigns more successful
- Achieve a quicker sale

Renovations with the Biggest Return*

Some home improvements will have a positive impact on the value of your home. The extent to which these home improvements affect your selling price will always be affected by the materials used and the quality of workmanship. It's important to keep in mind that in order for home improvements to achieve maximum impact on selling price, the updates must reflect the type of house being sold and the neighbourhood where the house is located. Unless major improvements are necessary, always try to keep updates to the simpler, less expensive variety.

The following is a list of the most common home improvement projects and the potential value that can be returned from the investment.

Highest Payback Potential	
Bathroom	75 – 100%
Kitchen	75 – 100%
Interior Painting	50 – 100%
Exterior Painting	50 – 100%
Average Payback Potential	
Roof Shingle Replacement	50 – 80%
Furnace/heating System	50 – 80%
Basement	50 – 75%
Recreation Room Addition	50 – 75%
Installing a Fireplace	50 – 75%
Flooring	50 – 75%
Constructing a Garage	50 – 75%
Window/door Replacement	50 – 75%
Building a Deck	50 – 75%
Central Air Conditioning	25 – 75%
Lowest Payback Potential	
Landscaping	25 – 50%
Interlocking Paving	25 – 50%
Building a Fence	25 – 50%
Asphalt Paving	20 – 50%
Adding a Swimming Pool	10 – 40%
Installing a Skylight	0 – 25%

* Appraisal Institute of Canada's 2004 Home Renovation Survey

Preparing Your Home to Sell

When selling your home, it is important to make a good first impression. Use the general guidelines below to ensure that your home is seen at its very best. The time you spend preparing your home will be well worth your effort and could ultimately help you get a better price, a quicker sale, or both.

Check the outside of your home for signs of wear and tear; peeling paint, loose shingles, hanging gutters, cracked foundation, holes in driveway; fix what's needed.

Cut the lawn, trim shrubs and rake the leaves from the yard.

Remove debris from gutters.

Make sure the front walk way is easy to access; remove leaves, snow, etc.

Ensure the entry way, stairs and hallways are not blocked with shoes, bags or other articles of clothing.

Repair and paint any walls, doors or casings that have marks or scuffs on them; always try and keep colors neutral; polish door knobs that are worn or faded.

Organize closets so they appear neat and tidy; store clothes that are out of season.

Make repairs to such things as leaky faucets, running toilets, etc.

Store kitchen appliances out of sight; make sure they are cleaned before storing.

Brighten up your rooms by switching to higher wattage light bulbs.

Clear out all of the clutter from your home and garage; if you don't use it regularly, throw it out or store it.

Air out your home to eliminate odors from carpets and drapes; light candles to fill the home with fresh aromas.

Remove personal items that may distract visitors from focusing on the home.

Seller's Self-Inspection Checklist

External Checklist	
Home Exterior	
__	Check all doors (house and garage), window frames and exterior trim for peeling paint; repaint or touch up as needed
__	Clear eaves troughs and gutters from debris
__	Ensure roof and shingles are in good repair
__	Make sure deck boards are in good condition
__	Clean the outside of all windows
__	Check all exterior plugs and water taps to make sure they are working
Yard / Driveway	
__	Mow the lawn; rake the leaves
__	Keep garden, flowers well pruned
__	Put away children's toys, bikes, etc.
__	Clean up after pets
__	Pick up any garbage lying around the yard
__	Make sure trash area is neat and organized
__	Repair driveway/walkways of spots and blemishes
__	Sweep walkways/driveway clear of dirt, twigs and grass
__	Ensure walkways, steps, and decks are free of obstacles, snow, etc.
__	Remove any unnecessary or extra lawn ornaments or furniture

Internal Checklist	
Entry / Stairs / Hallways	
__	Clear area of clutter: shoes, coats, bags, briefcases, etc.
__	Remove excess furniture such as coat racks, benches, book shelves, etc.
__	Vacuum or sweep floors
__	Keep area well lit
__	Clean windows, mirrors and picture frames
__	Repair any wall or door blemishes; paint chipping, marks, scuffs, etc.
__	Fix any wear and tear spots in the flooring

Kitchen / Bathrooms
__ Clean and store appliances in cupboards __ Wipe down counters and cupboards __ Organize cupboards __ Remove rust stains from sinks __ Make sure counter tops are free of clutter __ Ensure toilets and shower stalls are spotless __ Mop/scrub floors __ Lay out fresh towels, table cloths and curtains __ Make sure garbage cans are out of the way
Living Room / Family Room / TV Room
__ Dust lamps and furniture __ Vacuum, mop and/or sweep floors __ Clean all furniture in these rooms; make sure furniture is in good condition __ Make sure all light bulbs are working __ Put CDs, DVDs and video tapes away __ Put kids' toys away __ Ensure all bookshelves, entertainment systems and TV stands are free of dirt, dust and fingerprints __ Make sure plants are watered and in good shape; add new plants if necessary __ Clean all windows; make sure they open/close properly __ Ensure fireplace is clean and in working condition __ Store books, magazines and TV guides __ Find a place for all the remote controls __ Remove clutter of excess picture frames, ornaments, knick-knacks and furniture __ Rearrange furniture to maximize space and create spacious feeling
Bedrooms
__ Make sure beds are neatly made __ Ensure dirty laundry is in a laundry basket out of the way; cover laundry basket __ Clothes and footwear are put away neatly in the closet __ Closet is neatly organized __ Floor is swept, mopped or vacuumed __ Personal items are removed from the top of the dresser __ Clean all windows; ensure they open/close properly __ Dust all dresser tops __ Clean all mirrors __ Put kids' toys away

Garage / Basement / Storage	
__	Free of clutter
__	Well lit
__	Shelves clean and tidy
__	Boxes / storage units piled neatly
__	Floor is swept or vacuumed
__	Garbage is out of the way
__	Repair any blemishes/cracks/peeling on floor, wall, windows, etc.
__	Make sure room and equipment (furnace, air exchanger, humidifier, water heater, etc) are easy to access

General Checklist	
__	Ensure baseboards are clean and not faded; touch up with paint if necessary
__	Remove any cobwebs found throughout the house; check corners and doorways to infrequently used rooms
__	Repair any holes in the wall from wall hangings such as mirrors, pictures or ornaments
__	Check all plumbing for leaks
__	Replace or remove old, faded or ripped wall paper
__	Make sure all door handles/hinges and window latches work properly
__	Check all window/door screens to make sure they are in good condition
__	Repair any visible wiring

Showing Your Home

Once people realize your house is on the market, you are going to receive requests from buyers to view your home. The following best practices will help you get ready to show your home to these buyers:

Store valuables. Make sure items such as wallets, jewelry and loose money are put away and out of sight. While most buyers are only there to view the house, it's always better to have these types of personal belongings safely stored.

Minimize distractions. At the time of the showing keep the number of people in the house to a minimum. If possible, make arrangements to have the kids and pets out of the house while the buyers are going through it.

Create space. Experts suggest opening up curtains and turning on lights to help create a sense of space. Store excessive personal items such as pictures, frames, paintings, magazines, etc.; anything that is unnecessary and could contribute to buyer biases. The goal is to make the house less about you. You want buyers to be able to picture themselves living there.

Consider aroma. Baked goods, lightly scented candles, or potpourri can help create a delightful and inviting aroma in the house. Be careful to avoid strong or overbearing aromas as buyers could have allergies to these types of strong scents. Put out fresh towels. Remove your pet's favorite cushion, bed or litter box. Add fresh flowers or plants sparingly (avoid cluttering your home).

Have documents. Getting buyers to sign a guestbook is a good way to track the names and contact information of the people who have viewed your home. Have feature sheets – documents that explain the various features of the home – ready to hand out to the buyers. It's always a good idea to have supporting documents such as heating bills, electric bills, pool expenses and taxes handy in case the buyers are interested in these types of recurring expenses.

Be prepared. Make sure that you have enough time prior to the showing to tidy up any loose ends around the house. Make sure toys are put away, garbage is out of sight and pet areas are clean. There shouldn't be any clutter lying around the house. You want the buyers to focus on the features, not the flaws, of the house. Allow buyers to walk around the house by themselves, but be available to answer any questions they may have.

Negotiating Your Sale

Once you make the decision to sell your home privately, you should look at finding a real estate lawyer before you get too far into the sale process. Let the lawyer know of your intentions to sell privately and give him any details that you might find relevant to the sale.

The following is a list of considerations when approaching the negotiation process:

Select a real estate lawyer. It's important to secure the services of a real estate lawyer to represent your interests in the transaction. Ask your lawyer to go over the main clauses of a purchase and sale agreement so that you understand what will be involved in the negotiations. Remember, you would need to secure the services of a lawyer even if you were selling your home through an agent, so this should not be considered an extra expense. Some common questions have to do with timelines, deposits, conditions, adjustments, closing dates, etc. We strongly suggest you consult your lawyer on any legal questions you may have.

Know your rock bottom price. When you begin the process of selling privately, you will establish a price that you will ask for your home. Depending on factors such as the local housing market, time of year, urgency to sell, or other variables, some people will leave a little negotiation room when they set the price, but this isn't necessary. The key is to know what price you will ultimately accept for your home. If you do negotiate to cover certain costs as part of the sale, (such as upgrade allowances, costs of inspections, etc.), make sure you factor these into your bottom line price. Never divulge your lowest price during negotiations.

Not everyone will make an offer. Just because a buyer visits your home doesn't automatically mean they will present you with an offer. Since the home showing is typically a prospective buyer's first look at your property, they may realize after walking through that your home really isn't for them. Don't be discouraged by this. Think back to when you were shopping for your home; chances are you visited a number of homes before making your decision. Often, buyers will leave a home without providing any indication of interest but follow-up later to ask further questions.

Don't be surprised by any offer. Remember that buyers are trying to look out for their own interests in the negotiation process. Sometimes buyers will make a low-ball offer to see if the seller can be panicked into making a deal. As the seller, you can determine whether you want to submit a counter-offer. You may decide not to counter at all if you think that the buyer is not serious enough to continue negotiations.

Ask about mortgage pre-approval. Once you get buyers seriously interested in your property, make sure you ask them about their ability to pay for a home in your price range. You will want to make sure they have been pre-approved for a mortgage and that they have access to enough money to cover the purchase of your home. If they haven't yet been pre-approved, suggest to them that pre-approval should be their first step before they get too far along in negotiations.

Don't take things personally. Some buyers may try to characterize your home, or your view of your home, in not so flattering ways. By pointing out weaknesses, they are trying to strengthen their bargaining position. Don't let these types of tactics affect you. If you have done your proper research, searched for home comparisons or used an industry expert when setting your price, you can be confident in the price you set and recognize the tactic for what it is. Again, you can choose whether you want to continue negotiations or not.

Exchange lawyer information. When the foundations of a deal have been reached, exchange the names, addresses and phone numbers of the lawyers involved (i.e. your lawyer and the buyer's lawyer). Get the buyer to have his or her lawyer draft up the details of the purchase and sale agreement and have them sent to your lawyer's office. Putting this responsibility onto the buyer will help gauge the seriousness of the offer. Your lawyer will contact you to review the agreement. If there are any questions at this point, your lawyer can amend the agreement and send it to the buyer's lawyer for review. This process will continue until all the details are correctly accounted for within the agreement.

Include dates. When making offers and counter-offers, it's always a good idea to include timelines and dates for activities to occur. For example, the offer can be good for a certain number of days or a home inspection condition must be performed within a certain number of days from the date an agreement is signed. Mark each offer/counter-offer with date and time to prevent confusion as to which one is the most current. Including dates helps keep the process on track and sets deadlines for events to occur. Speak to your lawyer about reasonable time frames for conditions and all other activities that form part of the agreement.

Closing Your Sale

Once a deal is reached, you and the buyer must agree upon and include a closing date in the purchase and sale agreement. The closing date is the day that you get paid for the property and turn over your keys and deed to the buyer.

When **considering the appropriate closing date**, it's important to keep in mind the activities that both parties will need to perform to get ready to close the transaction. For example, the buyer may need to make mortgage arrangements while you may need to find another home or make arrangements to have your belongings moved and/or stored. The closing date must also allow the lawyers to complete their necessary duties such as performing title searches. Closing date time frames can be anything from weeks to months depending on the needs of you and the buyer.

A closing date **can either be a fixed date or a scheduled date** contingent on a certain activity being performed (i.e. a closing date could be set for 30 days after a home inspection takes place). The key to setting a closing date is allowing a reasonable amount of time for both parties to get their affairs in order. You may want to consult with your lawyer to get a sense of what needs to be done before finalizing this date. As with other parts of the purchase and sales agreement, the closing date is a clause that can be counter-offered and negotiated.

The closing date is also the date **used by lawyers to perform cost adjustments** on the property. Adjustments are essentially payments made to you by the buyer for things you already paid for. For example, if you prepaid your taxes, home fuel or utilities, then the buyer would need to pay you for the pro-rated amount that goes beyond your closing date. These costs would typically be outlined in your statement of adjustments.

Once a closing date is set, this is the **date that you need to have all your belongings out of the house** and have it ready for the new owners to move in. This means that if there are any conditions in the purchase and sales agreement that are your responsibility, you would need to have them resolved before closing. For example, part of the agreement might require you to replace a carpet or repair some items. The closing date would be your deadline to have these issues addressed. The buyer will be performing a walk through on the closing date to ensure the house is in proper condition.

Moving Checklist

Moving can be a hectic time. Below you'll find a checklist of activities that need to be performed as you get closer to your moving day.

While the list may not be exhaustive in your circumstance, it can be used as a guide to get you off on the right foot.

Leading up to Moving Day:
__ Book moving company or rental truck for the day before and the day of the move (you may need the truck longer depending on the distance you are moving).
__ If you are not moving directly into your new house, make arrangements for storing your belongings until the move-in date.
__ To ensure you don't get swamped days before the move, start packing less used items in the weeks leading up to the move.
__ Leave only essential items unpacked until the last day or so; all non-essential items should be packed ahead of time.
__ Make sure you set aside important items such as credit cards, check books and legal documents so that they don't get packed accidentally.
__ As you are packing, throw out broken items and donate unused items to charitable causes. This will reduce the number of boxes you will need to move.
__ Clearly label the contents of the boxes as you pack items in them; even better, include a room designation so that items can be unloaded to their proper location in your new home.
__ Notify utilities, service providers and subscription services of your new address (see Change of Address Checklist) and arrange for disconnection of existing services.
__ Thoroughly clean all rooms in the house; hire a cleaning service if your budget allows.

Moving Day:

- __ Because moving day will be very busy, make arrangements for the kids and pets to be cared for while the heavy lifting is being done.
- __ Double-check the interior of the house to make sure all items have been removed; look in closets, shelves and storage spaces.
- __ Gather all user manuals, guides and warranties and leave them clearly visible for the new owners.
- __ Take final meter readings for your records – water, electricity, gas, oil and any other metered services.
- __ Do a complete scan of the outside of the house; check behind bushes, under decks, in sheds, etc.
- __ Close and lock all doors and windows.
- __ Make sure all taps and faucets have been turned off.
- __ Turn off all lights as you leave the house.
- __ Turn down all thermostats.
- __ Leave house keys where the new owner can find them; label them for the new owners.

Change of Address Checklist

As you get set for moving day, there are a number of things you will want to do to prepare for the big day. Keep the following checklist handy so that you don't miss updating your records.

New Address:

Street: ____

City: ________________ Province: ________________________

Postal Code: _________________

General Notifications:

__ Post office – change of address cards; set up mail forwarding
__ Driver's license
__ Banking institution
__ Credit card companies (including department store cards)
__ Newspaper
__ Magazine subscriptions
__ Loyalty programs (i.e. reward cards)
__ Miscellaneous delivery services
__ Other: ____

__ Employer
__ Doctor
__ Dentist
__ Opticians
__ Veterinarian
__ Other: ____

Arrange for Insurance:

__ Insurance company – notify insurance broker of new address along with details of the new property; update policy as required

Company: ____________________ Phone #: ___________

Date called: ______________________________

Disconnect Utilities at Old Address:

__ Telephone company – notify of moving date to disconnect existing service

Company: ____________________ Phone #: ___________

Date called: ______________________________

__ Power / Hydro services – notify of moving date to disconnect existing service

Company: ____________________ Phone #: ___________

Date called: ______________________________

__ Water services – notify of moving date to disconnect existing service

Company: ____________________ Phone #: ___________

Date called: ______________________________

__ Cable company (television) – notify of moving date to disconnect existing service

Company: ____________________ Phone #: ___________

Date called: ______________________________

__ Oil/Gas Company – notify of moving date to disconnect existing service

Company: ____________________ Phone #: ___________

Date called: ______________________________

__ Other utility – notify of moving date to disconnect existing service; provide new address and moving date for activation

Company: ____________________ Phone #: ___________

Date called: ______________________________

Activate Utilities for New Address:

__ Telephone company – provide new address and moving date for activation

Company: ____________________ Phone #: ___________

Date called: ______________________________

__ Power / Hydro services – provide new address and moving date for activation

Company: ____________________ Phone #: ___________

Date called: ______________________________

__ Water services – provide new address and moving date for activation

Company: ____________________ Phone #: ___________

Date called: ______________________________

__ Cable company (television) – provide new address and moving date for activation

Company: ____________________ Phone #: ___________

Date called: ______________________________

__ Oil/Gas Company – provide new address and moving date for activation

Company: ____________________ Phone #: ___________

Date called: ______________________________

__ Other utility – provide new address and moving date for activation

Company: ____________________ Phone #: ___________

Date called: ______________________________

Endnote

1. “Home Seller Consumer Insights; 2002-2003” by Realty ViewPoint. The report concludes that people that sell their home on their own typically see 6% more in gross profits on the sale of a home. This number increases to 29% when commissions are included in the calculations. Also, people that sell their home on their own typically sell in 8.1 weeks, while real estate agents take, on average, 11.5 weeks to sell a home. These conclusions show statistical evidence that there is both a time and monetary benefit to selling a home privately.